Contents

Psychotherapy for Depression

T. Byram Karasu, M.D.

JASON ARONSON INC.
Northvale, New Jersey
London

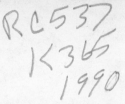

The author gratefully acknowledges permission to reprint the following:

Toward a Clinical Model of Psychotherapy for Depression, I: Systematic Approaches of Three Psychotherapies, by T. Byram Karasu, M.D. AMERICAN JOURNAL OF PSYCHIATRY, volume 147, pp. 133–145, February 1990. Copyright © 1990, the American Psychiatric Association. Reprinted by permission.

Toward a Clinical Model of Psychotherapy for Depression II: An Integrative and Selective Treatment Approach, by T. Byram Karasu, M.D. AMERICAN JOURNAL OF PSYCHIATRY, volume 147, pp. 269–278, March 1990. Copyright © 1990, the American Psychiatric Association. Reprinted by permission.

Library of Congress Cataloging-in-Publication Data

Karasu, Toksoz B.
    Psychotherapy for depression/T. Byram Karasu.
      p.   cm.
    Originally published as: The American journal of psychiatry. v.
147. no. 2-3
    Includes bibliographical references.
    ISBN 0-87668-691-9
    1. Depression, Mental.   2. Psychotherapy.   I. Title.
    [DNLM: 1. Depressive Disorder—therapy.   2. Psychotherapy—methods.
WM 171 K18p]
RC537.K365   1990
616.85'27—dc20
DNLM/DLC
for Library of Congress   90-1103
          CIP

Manufactured in the United States of America. Jason Aronson Inc. offers books and cassettes. For information and catalog write to Jason Aronson Inc., 230 Livingston Street, Northvale, New Jersey 07647.

1

Introduction

many effective models that can be utilized separately or together in order to locate the best therapeutic model for the future.

This book is intended to expand the repertoire of practitioners who may not be familiar with some of these approaches and also to provide a systematic delineation for better communication among them.

Preface

The content of this volume reflects the development of my thinking about a model for depression that would utilize the most current psychotherapeutic methods available in the field today. It also is directly in keeping with my overall philosophy of rapprochement, both within and across psychologic and pharmacologic domains.

More specifically, I view depression as a spectrum disorder with many faces. I believe that patients differ not only in the quantity and quality of that continuum, but also as individuals whose need for treatment must be considered along a wide range of variables. In light of the complexity of depressive disorders, any classification can be a simplistic reductionism, shortchanging the individual. Thus, greater respect for the individuality of the patient and his uniqueness may provide the best ethical and therapeutic guidelines for the well-informed practitioner.

Finally, my thesis here is that psychotherapy-responsive depression may be a self-correcting condition accelerated by various therapeutic approaches, in whole or in part. I have chosen only three of them because one is most commonly practiced (dynamic) and the other two (cognitive and interpersonal) most recently studied. I have no doubt that there are

**PART VII
PSYCHOTHERAPY AND PHARMACOTHERAPY:
A SELECTIVE AND INTEGRATIVE APPROACH**

**PART VIII
SELECTING PSYCHOTHERAPY
FOR INDIVIDUALIZED TREATMENT**

**PART IX
CONCLUSIONS**

ferred by its proponents. Despite increasing efforts to take a broader look at the current alternatives (10–12), such studies may be limited to a single basic contrast, such as psychoanalytic versus cognitive therapy (11), or may be incomplete— leaving direct comparisons implicit or not examining treatment that borrows central elements from different approaches (13).

This book is intended to begin to fill these two gaps. Part I will compare, on a variety of theoretical and technical dimensions, the three predominant psychotherapeutic approaches to depression today: psychodynamic, cognitive/ behavioral, and interpersonal. Then I will use these comparisons as the foundation for a treatment model that draws on both unique and shared elements of several perspectives.

From the 1930s to 1960s, the predominant therapies for major affective disorders were physical treatments and, of more controversial utility, traditional psychoanalysis (1). However, in the last two decades various psychosocial modalities have been increasingly used (with or without pharmacotherapy), and, perhaps equally crucial, their efficacy has been subjected to rigorous scientific study, which previously had been unavailable or inadequate (2). In particular, several new interventions, many short-term, have been expressly designed for depressive disorders (e.g., cognitive therapy, interpersonal therapy) or adapted to them (e.g., psychoanalytic or dynamic therapies) (3–7).

This increase in investigation has resulted in a wide array of psychological interventions, which are now part of the total treatment armamentarium for depression (8). While certain forms of depressive illness (e.g., bipolar mood disorder) still respond much better to somatic approaches (e.g., lithium), other types of depressive psychopathology can be successfully treated by psychological means (9). As in the larger field of psychiatry, however, pioneering descriptions of these options have typically tended to portray only one modality or approach and to involve only the form originated and/or pre-

Part I

PSYCHODYNAMIC APPROACH

2

Concepts of Pathology
and Etiology

The core conceptualizations of the etiology and pathogenesis of depression within a psychodynamic framework are rooted in Freud's general personality theories of infantile sexuality and intrapsychic conflict (14) and closely parallel some of the subsequent trends in overall psychoanalytic thinking (i.e., from instinct theory to ego and self psychology). In orthodox terms, depressive symptoms were originally viewed as a blockage of libido: when one is obliged to give up one's sexual aim without being gratified, he feels unloved and incapable of loving; consequently he despairs of himself and his future (15). Also observed in depressed patients was the same kind of ambivalence Freud (16) had earlier found in obsessional neurotic patients, in which hostility interferes with the capacity to love. A model of regression based on Freud's stages of psychosexual development was likewise applied to depression; unresolved conflict at the oral phase was considered directly related to the excessive need and subsequent search for oral gratification and to an unconscious wish to destroy (i.e., devour) the desired but frustrating sexual object (17).

An extension of his work on narcissism (18), the classic Freudian treatise specifically on depression is "Mourning and

Melancholia'' (19), which compares normal grief with pathological depression. The former is regarded as a reaction to the
loss of an external object (i.e., actual death), whereas in the
melancholic patient "the object has not perhaps actually died
but has been lost as an object of love." The major intrapsychic
consequence is an impoverished ego insofar as it becomes
identified with the lost object. For Freud there were thus
"three preconditions of melancholia—loss of the object, ambivalence, and regression of libido into the ego." In short, the
person's anger and disappointment are turned inward toward
himself instead of toward the real object, for whom his
aggression is meant; it is presumed that henceforth a repressed rage (aggressive cathexes in place of libidinal cathexes) underlies the depressed affect. On the basis of traditional psychoanalytic theory, Abraham (20) gradually
formulated five factors in the pathogenesis of melancholia: a
constitutional overemphasis on oral eroticism, fixation of
psychosexual development at the oral stage, early and repeated childhood disappointments in love, occurrence of first
major developmental disappointment before oedipal wishes
are resolved, and repetition of primary disappointment in
later life. Further tracing the theme of separation and loss
(both real and perceived), later studies of acute grief in adults
(21, 22) have confirmed Freud's observations and the many
features that grief shares with pathological depression; they
also highlight significant symptoms not seen in normal bereavement, including functional impairment, suicidal ideation, and overwhelming feelings of worthlessness (23).

   Subsequent dynamic theory largely shifted to the importance of object relations and development of self, especially
the issues involving self-esteem and its determinants. As a
conceptual bridge toward psychological predisposition
(rather than constitution), Rado (24) stressed the dependence
of the depressive person's self-esteem on narcissistic supplies
outside the self, describing the motive as a "great despairing

cry for love." Klein (25) hypothesized a period of great ambivalence called "the depressive position," marked not only by fear of loss of love but by guilt about desire for the hated object, which if not resolved predisposes the child to later depression. Fenichel (26) suggested that the depressive person sustained a narcissistic injury in early childhood (i.e., traumatic disappointment in parental affection) whereby self-esteem and love became equated and that the entire depressive process is an attempt to repair the damaged ego. Bibring's radical view of depression (27), as a fundamental ego state, involved consolidation of all depressive phenomena into a loss of self-esteem, and he postulated that different unresolved psychosexual stages lead to different types of depression. Thenceforth, the theoretical tide has increasingly turned away from psychoanalytic metapsychology to notions of depression as a basic affect, and from loss of a love object to the more global erosion of a sense of well-being (28).

3

Current Directions

3

Current Directions

In her more than 25 years of work with the ego psychology of depressive persons, Jacobson (29) has established loss of self-esteem as their central psychological problem and exaggerated dependency as a specific ego weakness, and she has carefully examined the nature of ego regression in the depressive patient by delineating several intrapsychic determinants of this fragile self-esteem: superego impairment (very harsh), faulty ego ideal (unrealistic or grandiose idealized love objects), pathological development of self-representations (devalued or distorted body image), immature and self-critical ego functions, and, in severe pathology, the dissolution of all these structures. Kohut's theories on the formation and restoration of the self (30, 31), albeit not directed primarily at depressive illness, have placed in bold relief the need for empathic self-objects in the development of normal self-esteem and the impact of early attachment issues on later problems in separation-individuation. He suggested that when the self is seriously damaged or destroyed, the child turns away from unempathic or absent self-objects to escape depression. Deprivation of idealized self-objects, for example, can result in "empty" depression (depletion of self-esteem and vitality) or "guilt" depression (uncurbed self-rejection and self-blame).

Current theoretical concepts incorporate some of the classic and later ego analytic and self constructs. Like other psychopathology, depression is considered the consequence of underlying conflict, and emphasis is placed on the influence of the past on present object relationships—specifically, excessive reliance on limited external sources of gratification for a sense of worth. In regard to the latter, Arieti (32) discerned two basic patterns of depressive personality organization—"dominant other" (the depressive person relies solely on another person) and "dominant goal" (the external source of esteem is the fulfillment of some great ambition). Both types are founded on the childhood development of a maladaptive way of bolstering the sense of self (27).

In summary, modern dynamic theory now combines, to greater or lesser degrees, such psychoanalytic formulations as early childhood disappointment and loss (which predispose to later depression), damaged self-esteem arising from a marked discrepancy between the actual self and ego ideal, persistence of narcissistic rage beneath an unloved and punished self, omnipotent wishes that both tenuously support and defensively fend off a sense of helplessness and hopelessness, and difficulties in autonomy and intimacy due to reactivation of intrapsychic conflicts about these unsettled issues arising in infancy (33). This largely unconscious matrix forms the foundation for subsequent depressive episodes through repetition of childhood experiences with significant others; this reiteration of earlier patterns is manifested in a breakdown of the intrapsychic processes that maintain self-esteem. These theoretical assumptions have remained essentially intact despite revisions of the concepts regarding the precise nature of unresolved remnants from childhood that are carried to adulthood (i.e., historically, these remnants were initially attributed to repressed real events, subsequently to forbidden fantasies, and most recently, to persistent erroneous beliefs) (3). Moreover, these assumptions continue to underlie current dynamic treatment, despite significant technical differences between long-term and short-term modalities (33).

4

Primary Tools and Practices

Three background issues are relevant to the use of psychodynamic techniques in depression.

1. Psychodynamic techniques, derived from psychoanalysis, were originally developed for general application to neurotic personality structure, not for treating specific depressive symptoms. Thus, direct applications to major depression have been relatively sparse (3, 29, 34).

2. Because the psychoanalytic approach has evolved over nearly a century, it now encompasses a varied spectrum of schools and strategies, ranging from classical open-ended formats (35) to contemporary time-limited ones (36–39) and including modifications that are both extrinsic (e.g., reduced frequency) and intrinsic (e.g., greater emphasis on the here-and-now) (40, 41).

3. Because of the historical variations in individual schools and techniques and the long-standing difficulties in standardization of the art of analysis, dynamic practices have only begun to be defined and operationalized in treatment manuals (6, 7).

The primary psychodynamic strategies are insight-oriented and include confrontation (evocative questioning), clarification (elaboration or sharper focus), interpretation (the sine qua non of dynamic treatment: assignment of underlying meaning or cause to a feeling or behavior), and working through (continual integration of the entire interpretive process). These techniques are essentially designed to facilitate analysis of transference and resistance—exploration of the ongoing therapist-patient relationship and obstacles to it by means of projecting past positive and negative feelings toward significant figures onto the current interpersonal situation (35). Luborsky's principles of psychoanalytic psychotherapy (7) are based on the need to formulate and reformulate the patient's main relationship problems in the context of the underlying transference relationship so as to derive a core conflictual relationship theme; this motif covers all three of the patient's relationship spheres: past, current in-treatment, and current out-of-treatment. Strupp and Binder's time-limited dynamic psychotherapy (6) uses a "focal narrative" to address repeated problems of living based on real or imagined interpersonal transactions.

Recent descriptions of the changes in psychodynamic treatment theory and practice since Freud's time portray a spectrum of expressive and supportive techniques, although traditionally they have been regarded as antithetical (41). Strupp et al. (33) have suggested that while the underlying assumptions are identical, modern techniques differ from traditional dynamic practices in three major ways: (a) shorter treatment duration, the crucial factor, which is often a direct function of the depth or extent of therapist goals (symptomatic versus characterological change), (b) a more active role on the part of the therapist (direct versus reflective stance), and (c) a more vigorous approach (confronting defenses and clarifying present problems versus interpreting core conflicts). Specific treatment variations include Sifneos's short-term anxiety-provoking psychotherapy (36), which, like long-term analysis, focuses on original oedipal conflict and uses transference interpretations as its major tool; Davanloo's highly confrontational approach (38), in which transference is interpreted in terms of childhood experiences and therapist-parent links are made but the primary modus operandi is persistent challenge of defensive behaviors involved in the patient's resistance to human alliance; and Mann's time-limited psychotherapy (37), which uses a pre-set finite period in which to examine preoedipal and oedipal development in terms of the patient's unconscious experience of time.

The application of psychodynamic techniques to treatment of depression entails careful examination, within an essentially closed dyadic system, of the depressed patient's unrealistic responses to the therapist as the patient replays early disappointment in parental affection, attempts to gain lost love, and makes specific self-protective maneuvers that obstruct therapeutic progress. Particular ego distortions (e.g., excessive ego ideals) and superego defects (e.g., unduly harsh conscience) are the structural intrapsychic foci for exploration (29). Especially in the initial phase of treatment, the therapist may confront defenses and pathological patterns of behavior (e.g., idealization, manipulativeness, clinging dependency) in the depressive patient's attempts to gain magical relief and reinstate self-esteem (42). In fact, many now believe that confrontation of negative transference is essential from the very beginning (6, 36, 38). Using a nonanalytic measure, the dynamic therapist may also encourage cathartic release of repressed aggressive affect, which is presumed to underlie the depressive disorder (43). This method does not directly facilitate insight but can be at least temporarily therapeutic, since anger is expressed toward the therapist as a substitute for early frustrating figures. Recent clinical observations indicate that short-term psychodynamic strategies for depression may also vary but have in common four successive stages of treatment (34).

1. During *primary resistance* to the formation of a therapeutic alliance, in which the depressed patient is fending off

primary loss in response to early parental separation, the therapist may challenge and clarify the patient's unresolved ambivalence toward his parents.

2. During *treatment resistance*, the beginning of defensive reactions against the therapy process itself, the therapist continually interprets the depressive patient's repeated self-defeating behavior and fears of retaliation.

3. During *termination resistance*, in which the patient starts to sense impending separation from the therapist and remobilizes earlier irrational reactions to loss, the therapist often must deal with the open expression of anger.

4. By *termination resolution*—the depressed patient's relatively realistic grief over the loss of the therapist—therapist techniques are consolidated in a continual process of working through core conflicts by means of resolving current ones, both within and outside the therapy sessions.

5

Therapeutic Relationship
and Therapist Role

The formation of a transferential relationship to explore unconscious repetition of defensive and adaptive coping patterns formed in the past is the hallmark of the dynamic approach. Brief dynamic therapies are based on a modified transference paradigm (33), in which the current therapeutic relationship is an in vivo expression of the patient's problems with relatedness. The establishment of a trusting working alliance (33) for realistic interaction between partners is the foundation of the ensuing transference process. Here the therapist's major role is as an interpreter/reflector (44); this role includes such features as a primarily receptive attitude (principle of evenly suspended attention), neutral acceptance ("blank screen"), and relative frustration (rule of abstinence) (35). These practices have altered, however, and are now more flexible, especially in terms of the therapist's directness and activity (6). Therapist silence, classically used to facilitate free association and regression, may be applied occasionally to encourage transference formation in attempts to tap more repressed material. This practice is embedded in receptive listening, which prevails throughout treatment.

Luborsky (7) delineated the dynamic therapist's expressive-supportive role. The expressive aspect has four phases:

the therapist listens receptively, understands, responds, and returns to listening while bearing in mind the patient's reaction to his previous response. The basic attitude is expectant and involves both observing and experiencing (33), which requires that the therapist be acutely attentive to the patient so that he can resonate with the patient's feelings and be aware of his own emotions. The supportive stance involves maintaining the patient's experience of a helping alliance by conveying empathy and nonjudgmental respect for the patient and by communicating realistic hope. These therapist attitudes are the means for establishing a therapeutic alliance and transference relationship of benign dependency, through which positive and negative transference and extratransference manifestations are confronted, clarified, and worked through in the here-and-now.

6

Major Goals and Mechanisms of Change

Belief in insight as the primary psychodynamic mechanism of change is based on the philosophy that the unexamined life repeats itself; the patient returns to more regressed patterns of behavior as long as unconscious intrapsychic conflicts remain repressed—unremembered, unrevealed, and therefore unresolved (45). The depressive patient's response to past experiences of loss or failure is unexpressed feelings related to his injured ego (repressed hostility, ambivalence toward significant others), which persist until he gains understanding and works through narcissistic cravings for love (29). The symptoms of depression are thought to subside as the patient brings to the surface his pervasive disappointment in parental affection and approval stemming from childhood or, in shorter-term approaches, as the patient comprehends scenarios within treatment that reiterate comparable current relations to significant others (3, 6, 7). In particular, the depressed patient is helped to recognize the latent meaning of his special vulnerability to loss of self-esteem and the excessiveness of his demands, which are related to pervasive feelings of sadness, guilt, and unworthiness (29). Of course, this process occurs within the context of a transferential and empathic relationship between therapist and patient, in which the therapist becomes a role model who represents both an old and new object (46).

In addition, as the patient recounts early or recent memories and experiences, he can conciously examine the defensive and/or adaptive part that depressed affect plays in keeping repressed aggression at bay (43). This may accompany more immediate therapeutic change during dynamic therapy, i.e., cathartic relief through confession of unexpressed feelings. However, the latter method has been criticized as overused in psychodynamic practice, a carryover of the theoretical equation of aggression and depression in earlier psychodynamic thinking (43). It also is anachronistic in that it predates the significant transition in analytic thinking from catharsis to insight as the crucial agent of change (35).

As old modes of behavior are interpreted and clarified, the patient better understands his self-defeating way of attempting to gain self-esteem, excessive expectations of nurturance, need for proof of love and praise by idealized others, disappointment in parental affection, and consequent sense of failure and fears of abandonment. As insights are incorporated into his life over time in and outside of therapy, they can gradually form a permanent foundation for preventing future depressive episodes. That is, with some resolution of conflictual feelings, the patient can search for more gratifying, realistic ways to achieve a sense of worth.

The psychodynamic approach—whether long- or short-term—thus aims to modify the structural substrate of the depressive disorder, not merely its immediate manifestations. Resolving intrapsychic conflict related to significant others in the patient's present and past effects a reorganization of ego and superego structures, not simply symptomatic relief (29). More specifically, the psychodynamic model may be regarded as having several successive goals for the depressive patient, which are in part contingent on length of treatment: (a) to

provide symptom relief through cathartic expression of sup-
pressed aggressive feelings, (b) to lower superego demands
and perfectionistic standards so as to reduce feelings of guilt
and inadequacy, thus allowing self-esteem to be raised, (c) to
make clear how current narcissistic wishes for love and
excessive expectations in significant relationships are unrealistic and misdirected, i.e., how they are unwittingly repeated
in actions toward others and aggressively turned against the
self, and (d) to uncover and recreate the earlier conflicts from
which the current disorder derives (3, 29, 43).

Part II

COGNITIVE APPROACH

7

Concepts of Pathology and Etiology

7

Concepts of Pathology
and Etiology

The major historical roots of the cognitive approach to depression can be traced from first-century Greek Stoicism and ancient Eastern religion to two modern influences of the twentieth century: phenomenology and its once ardent adversary, behaviorism. The early Stoics believed that a wise man is free from passion, unmoved by grief or joy, and submissive to natural law, and they were among the first to contend that the control of intense feelings could be accomplished by altering one's ideas. Epictetus (55–135 A.D.), a proponent of this stance in Rome, forecast the cognitive concept of pathology in his succinct statement "Men are disturbed not by things but by the views which they take of them."

Although Freud (45) did initially present the thesis that affect and symptoms are founded in unconscious ideas, i.e., mental representations of physiologic excitations, Adler's school of individual psychology was instrumental in applying the view that repressed experiences, such as infantile sexual traumas, are less significant than the patient's own self-determined, conscious perceptions of these events; Adler named this personal representation of external reality the "phenomenal field" (47). The behaviorist tradition was superimposed on these phenomenologic premises, with its theoretic emphasis on environmental learning, and its technical use of conscious control in the modification of behavior. A crucial transition, however, was the shift from classical conditioning to an information processing behavioral model, i.e., from an emphasis on actions to stress on cognitions (48). On the American front, Kelly's psychology of personal constructs (49) was a specific therapeutic approach designed to alter patients' conscious experience; his fixed role technique, for example, has the patient assume a role incongruent with his typical assumptions about himself and his world and, by so doing, confront the erroneous personal constructs that are damaging his life. In a comparable vein, Ellis's rational-emotive therapy (50) directly attacks irrational false beliefs; his ABC theory involves intervention of a person's beliefs (B) between an activating environmental event (A) and its emotional consequences (C).

While several theorists have since contributed to the cognitive-behavioral framework and its application to psychopathology, the culminating developments in the cognitive approach to depressive disorders occurred over a decade and a half (1963–1979) of systematic clinical observations and experimental testing by Beck, Rush, and their associates (4). Initial impetus for the application of their cognitive thesis about depression came from experimental investigations of the dreams of depressive patients: instead of yielding Freudian unconscious, wish-fulfilling, masochistic content full of repressed rage and guilt, the dreams revealed repetitive themes of rejection, disappointment, and injury that matched the patients' conscious views when they were awake. Moreover, such self-deprecating cognitive constructs about individual patients proved objectively false, i.e., independent of empirical evidence (51).

8

Current Directions

Currently, the major guidelines to the use and validation of a cognitive model in the treatment of depression are the work of Beck and associates (4). In essence, Beck's cognitive theory of depression posits that negatively distorted thinking patterns (ideas and images) are the basis for depressed behavior and symptoms; in short, dysphoria is a disturbance of cognition, not mood. Beck and associates expressly pointed out that such a theory addresses not ultimate etiology (such as hereditary disposition or faulty learning) but, rather, how maladaptions in cognitive structure, i.e., defective information processing mechanisms, predispose the individual to depressive disorder (4).

It is now theorized that there are three central maladaptive elements of depressive psychopathology: (a) a cognitive triad of recurrent negative views, which directly shape how the person sees himself, the world, and the future, (b) implicit irrational schemata based on the past by which the individual personally gathers, translates, and labels experiences, and (c) logical errors that pervade the assessment of one's self and life events. The cognitive triad comprises self-concept distortions (e.g., pronounced evaluation of oneself as deficient, defective, and/or undeserving), an overestimation of the environment (e.g., as unduly demanding, depriving, and/or rejecting), and a pessimistic view of the future (e.g., as without promise, value, or meaning). The other two characteristics considered essential to the maintenance of depressive symptoms, silent assumptions and logical errors, accompany this fundamental triad and compound its dysfunctional effects. Silent assumptions are rigidly held, covert, nonverbal axioms (usually misconceptions about love, approval, achievement, and the like) from which depressive persons draw their negative conclusions (e.g., If I don't win X's love, I am unworthy; If disappointing event X occurs in my presence, it's my fault; If goal X is denied me once, it will never be mine). Integral to these assumptions are errors in logic, which lead to irrational and exaggerated deductions. These faulty reasoning processes include selective attention, i.e., perceiving and focusing on certain dark features of an event while overlooking others; overgeneralization, i.e., using a solitary incident as the basis of sweeping conclusions about one's self and the future; and personalization, i.e., considering oneself the central or causative agent in events for which one is not realistically responsible. Such cognitive experiences are regarded as idiosyncratic to depression in both process as well as content, in that they are invariably automatic, persistent, and devoted to the overriding theme of loss (52).

9

Primary Tools and Practices

9

Primary Tools and Practices

Cognitive therapy is standardized and brief (15–20 interviews) and is characterized by highly specific learning experiences; each session consists of a review of reactions to and results of the previous session, planning, specific tasks, and assignment of homework (4). The major modus operandi of the cognitive approach is logical analysis (12), application of the basic principles of logic and experimental investigation (i.e., data collection, inductive questioning, hypothesis formation, prediction, postulation of alternative explanations, and validation in reality) to the automatic tenets by which the depressed patient perceives, organizes, and responds to the world around him. Each persistent negative construct that accompanies depressed affect (e.g., I am a bad person; Nobody likes me; I am going to fail) is identified, its frequency and circumstances are noted, and it is posed as a specific testable hypothesis to which rules of reason are applied and for which evidence is gathered from everyday events (4).

To initially orient and involve the patient, he is assigned concrete reading material on coping with depression (53) and written self-reports (a weekly activity schedule to chart tangible behaviors, a mastery and pleasure schedule to rank degree of gratification and accomplishment). Both counteract initial passivity and demonstrate a direct way for depressed individuals to begin to gain greater control over their lives, i.e., by planning more productive activities.

Thereafter, special cognitive strategies help the patient to (a) detect, record, and review depressogenic beliefs identified in the patient's daily record of dysfunctional thoughts and deduce distorted assumptions, (b) recognize the relationship between irrational cognitions and self-defeating experiences, using concrete examples from recent events, (c) locate recurrent themes, such as fear of failure and the need to be perfect, through explicit assistance in categorization, (d) correct these perceptions by conducting mini-projects of progressive difficulty ("graded task assignments") (M.R. Goldfried, personal communication, 1979), (e) find explanations of events that are more rational and positive by using reattribution techniques, which challenge the depressed patient's dominant axiom of total responsibility for adverse occurrences, and ultimately, (f) progressively develop more adaptive and gratifying thinking patterns through repeated logical analysis, collection of evidence, and trial application in real-life situations. In addition, assertiveness training, role playing, and cognitive rehearsal (modeling and practice through dramatization or imagination) enable the patient to actively master specific scenarios, which serve as models for real-life achievement.

10

Therapeutic Relationship and Therapist Role

The term "collaborative empiricism" has been coined to characterize the major therapeutic relationship in cognitive therapy, in which "the therapist is continually active and deliberately interacting with the patient" (4, p. 6). The two participants have been further depicted as an investigative team; the content of each depressed thought is posed as a hypothesis to be tested by two scientists, who collect all the evidence in order to support or refute that hypothesis (12).

To foster a rational collaboration, the cognitive therapist gives special attention to openly preparing the patient for what will transpire each step of the way, with explicit instruction and supplementary reading. Since the patient's active participation may be at least initially compromised by the depressive symptoms (e.g., lack of energy or motivation, difficulties in concentration), the therapist also engages the patient by gaining his explicit agreement to the treatment plan and thereafter involves him in specific tasks. This engagement includes joint selection of a target problem and continual feedback throughout the treatment (e.g., constant inquiry as to the patient's reactions, written appraisals of each session for postsession review) (12).

Under the collaborative empiricism model, the major role

of the therapist is primarily educative (4, p. 404)—to instruct and advise the patient in rational thinking and to provide active guidance during systematic reality testing, which is considered intrinsic to the cognitive approach. The therapist actively points out automatic thoughts, helps to identify cognitions from the patient's report of recent experiences, reviews patient records, assigns homework, and provides concrete feedback. Often part of this tutorial approach is a direct problem-solving question-and-answer format, with which the therapist and patient can jointly explore the patient's cognitions. Although the therapist is thus a "teacher/ shaper," a descriptor that characterizes the overall behavioral model of psychotherapy (44), with depressed patients he especially avoids authoritarian acts, such as interrogation or manipulation, which can exacerbate feelings of inadequacy and powerlessness. In Young and Beck's terms (54), it is a process of discovery, not persuasion.

In fact, because it is considered crucial to minimize negative responses, to which depressed persons are particularly prone, the therapist attempts to maintain a positive alliance at all times. By implicitly employing positive transference elements, he thus diffuses or avoids the development of irrational transference, which can lead to disappointment or dysphoric reactions. Such responses are not always avoidable, and they are dealt with immediately through conscious mutual examination: the patient writes down all the characteristics attributed to the therapist, and the patient and therapist jointly scrutinize their content logically, as with any other cognitive distortion.

11

Major Goals and Mechanisms of Change

Whereas in typical behavior modification alterations in overt behavior are viewed as an end in themselves, with the cognitive approach they are considered a means to cognitive change (4, p. 4). The goals of this approach have been succinctly stated by its originators: "to teach the patient the following operations: (a) to monitor his negative, automatic thoughts (cognitions); (b) to recognize the connections between cognition, affect, and behavior; (c) to examine the evidence for and against his distorted automatic thought; (d) to substitute more reality-oriented interpretations for these biased cognitions; and (e) to learn to identify and alter the dysfunctional beliefs which predispose him to distort his experiences" (4, p. 4).

The major cognitive aims or processes of change have three successive components: recognition of faulty thinking through self-monitoring, modification of thinking patterns through systematic evaluation and empirical testing of the validity of automatic thoughts and silent assumptions, and self-mastery by means of homework and everyday practice on one's own (8).

The initial phase of treatment, which aims at symptom reduction, emphasizes the recognition of self-destructive thoughts, whereas the subsequent phases, which aim at prophylaxis, concentrate on the modification of specific erroneous assumptions within and outside the treatment sessions. To isolate, control, and change illogical thinking—the cognitive concept of cure—treatment is organized to elicit and subject to rational examination the actual mental contents of conscious depressive ideation (current automatic thoughts, silent assumptions, attitudes, values, daydreams) and to trace their impact on dysphoric feelings and behaviors in current concrete situations. Its ultimate purpose is self-control and self-mastery—the patient explicitly rehearses and trains himself to recognize and restructure his own faulty cognitions so he can cope better in the future.

Part III

INTERPERSONAL APPROACH

12

Concepts of Pathology
and Etiology

Although the interpersonal approach to depressive disorder subscribes to a pluralistic point of view (i.e., the belief that no single cause in itself can explain depression) (5, p. 38), it is nonetheless founded on the hypothesis that the crucial factor in depression is the social network or interpersonal milieu of the patient. More specifically, it holds that disturbed social roles and unsatisfactory interpersonal relationships (especially the absence or loss of significant others) in childhood and/or adulthood can be antecedents to and/or consequences of depressive disorders and can play a part in both causal and risk factors (3).

The beginnings of the interpersonal model of pathology and treatment were largely the theoretical contributions of the Swiss-born psychiatrist Adolf Meyer and his American associate at Johns Hopkins, Harry Stack Sullivan. Meyer's innovative psychobiology (55) was pivotal in its application of the Darwinian concept of biological adaptation (56) to the understanding of psychiatric disorders; such a disorder was seen in terms of social adaptation, as the consequence of the individual's attempts to adapt to his surroundings. Early developmental experiences, especially family and environmental influences, were construed as the critical factors in the person's subsequent responses to the events around him. Sullivan (57) went further in concretizing these ideas; the Washington school of psychiatry represented an interpersonal approach that applied the cultural context of personality development to the arena of clinical psychiatry, drawing from anthropology, sociology, and social psychology. It was distinctive in viewing psychiatry as the scientific study of interpersonal relations (which challenged the basic Freudian concept of an instinctual sexual and intrapsychic basis for psychopathology). Although many of the founders and proponents of this approach (e.g., Frieda Fromm-Reichmann, Karen Horney, Erich Fromm, and Sullivan himself) had originally been trained in psychoanalysis and did not necessarily reject such fundamental analytic constructs as the unconscious or the major role of childhood experiences, they placed much greater emphasis on social, cultural, and familial factors than on biological or dynamic internal forces.

13

Current Directions

The Washington school laid the groundwork for the interpersonal approach to depression by shifting away from social psychiatric approaches that focused on large units of culture or society and on macroscopic environmental events, such as urbanization or the influence of social class. Rather, the unit of observation became the "primary social group, the immediate face-to-face involvement of the patient with one or more significant others" (5, p. 47). More specifically, it focuses on the individual's social circle, the most intimate family and love relationships, friendship, work, and community impact. The current interpersonal approach also stems from an assortment of research investigations with important implications for the study of depression: ethologic and experimental research in animal behavior, developmental studies of childhood, epidemiological surveys, and clinical investigations of adult psychopathology. These include the series of studies of mother-child and other attachment bonds (58–60), research on the relation of external life events to stress (61, 62), community surveys regarding the role of intimacy (63), and with the most direct implications, clinical explorations of the social relations of depressed adult patients (64).

The empirical findings from these studies highlight some

65

of the basic concepts associated with this model: (a) the developmental importance of attachment or affectional bonds in depression—that is, the vulnerability of individuals to problematic interpersonal relations and psychiatric disorders if solid maternal bonds are not established early in life (58, 65)—and the relation of weak social bonds to depression (66, 67), (b) the notion of intimacy as protection against depression (63, 68, 69), (c) the relationship between recent stressful life events and the onset of depression (70, 71), and (d) the concordance between deterioration in all aspects of social functioning—e.g., poor communication, disruption of marriage or other major relationship—and the appearance of clinical depression (72, 73).

Childhood antecedents can be as specific as the actual absence or death of a parent early in life or, more likely, negative experiences related to the loss (5); childhood exposure to abuse, neglect, or family discord (74); and history of affective illness in the family (5). Similarly, adult antecedents include current social stressors (61), especially chronic marital discord, divorce, and separation (75).

In short, one's social bonds, their quality (how supportive) more than their quantity, are crucial to the individual's total adaptation and susceptibility to depression. The interpersonal approach thus places high priority, during illness and health, on the presence of gratifying intimate relationships with others and positive communication, primarily in marital and family relations but also in work, school, and peer relations (5). The most recent representation of this approach is Klerman et al.'s interpersonal therapy (5), which specifically recognizes four major interpersonal areas or problems that are commonly associated with major depression: (a) abnormal grief reaction, i.e., severe or unusual bereavement in response to the death of a significant other, (b) interpersonal role disputes, i.e., unreasonable, nonreciprocal expectations of or by significant others, especially disagreements about sex roles, (c) difficult role transitions—unsuccessful attempts to cope with developmental landmarks or with significant life events (positive or negative), such as getting married or divorced, having a child, graduating from school, changing careers, or retiring—and (d) interpersonal deficits, including inadequate social skills and history of social isolation or transient relationships.

14

Primary Tools and Practices

14

Primary Tools and Practices

The interpersonal approach shares elements with both the psychodynamic and cognitive approaches and is, by the admission of its own proponents, not a new form of treatment (5). It emphasizes the solving of interpersonal problems and entails supportive and behavioral strategies as well as both directive and non-directive exploratory methods—information, guidance, reassurance, clarification, communication skills education, behavioral modification, and environmental management. Didactic educational techniques and environmental interventions are largely used in the initial efforts to ameliorate overt symptoms, whereas support, exploration, behavioral modification, and social skills training are subsequently applied to specific interpersonal issues.

The first phase of interpersonal treatment, which focuses on the immediate depressive symptoms, includes information gathering and assessment for both the therapist and patient. The therapist may use a structured interview (e.g., Schedule for Affective Disorders and Schizophrenia, Diagnostic Interview Schedule) that focuses on current life events and family history, especially events related to the depressive episode, and confirm these findings with explicit diagnostic queries to the patient.

The patient is also given direct information about depression as a clinical condition, often with the instruction to read recommended literature written in lay language (76). These efforts are all ultimately directed at legitimizing the sick role of the patient. This intentional, temporary therapeutic stance expresses the explicit alliance of interpersonal therapy with the medical model and is an important aspect of therapeutic improvement. (This does not, however, preclude the simultaneous minimization of dependency with suggestions that the patient engage in work and social activities whenever possible.) During the first phase the therapist also assesses current interpersonal relationships and the specific problem area to be addressed. The formation of a therapeutic contract is another goal of the first phase and provides the patient with an explicit treatment plan. This phase entails essentially didactic discussion, supportive exploration, and management of the patient's immediate interpersonal environment.

The middle phase, which is the crux of treatment, addresses the identified primary problem area. Each of the four hypothesized basic problems has its own therapeutic tasks and strategies in the here-and-now. For example, in dealing with abnormal grief reactions, a major technique is facilitation of the mourning process to allow expression and exploration of affects surrounding the loss, both positive and negative—sadness, guilt, and remorse, as well as good feelings, courage, and hope for new beginnings. This provides not only cathartic relief but a broader perspective, an alternative way of looking at the lost relationship. At the same time, the therapist is supportively offered as a temporary object who substitutes for the lost person until real replacements can be fostered through new involvements outside of therapy and the acquisition of additional social skills and interests.

In dealing with interpersonal role disputes, whether they involve marital, parental, employment, or peer networks, identification of the disagreement relating to the depression is the initial task and includes locating the predominant stage of the role dispute—complete dissolution, temporary impasse, or amenability to renegotiation (5). Here the patient is encouraged to examine maladaptive perceptions, faulty communications, and nonreciprocal expectations that are exacerbating the problem, as the therapist helps to clarify them and guide the patient into new ways of relating to others and alternative interpersonal behaviors. This often entails communication analysis and training in new communication skills.

In addressing a role transition, the therapist may have to deal with the patient's equation of significant life changes with loss; the patient's response to such developmental events or alterations is like a grief reaction. A major strategy, however, is to assist the patient in distinguishing such events from real losses and to guide him in abandoning the old roles and preparing for new interpersonal tasks. Here the emphasis is on a larger repertoire of social skills and on interpersonal mastery, which will improve the patient's adaptation to the demands of his current roles. The theme with such role transitions, as in abnormal grief, is the use of losses as opportunities for new possibilities and growth.

Interpersonal deficits generally involve lack of the experience and interpersonal skills required to initiate or sustain relationships. Although severe social isolation may represent a more serious disturbance, many of the interpersonal problems of depressive patients can be altered through clarification of the positive and negative aspects of relationships, social skills training, and other behavioral modification techniques. In each instance, a positive relationship with the therapist can serve as a model and provide practice for future relationships during the ongoing negotiation of problematic interpersonal scenarios during therapy.

15

Therapeutic Relationship and Therapist Role

According to its originators, the therapeutic relationship in interpersonal therapy is explicitly "not . . . the primary focus of treatment" (5, p. 149). Nonetheless, the role of the therapist and use of the therapeutic relationship have been delineated according to the following major guidelines.

1. The therapist is an advocate of the patient, not neutral. The therapist's essential role is as a benign and helpful ally who is basically supportive while offering direct advice and reassurance.

2. The interpersonal therapist takes a deliberately directive stance, but in actual practice it represents a moderate position between highly active and highly reactive; the therapeutic role is both prescriptive and exploratory.

3. The therapeutic relationship is not interpreted as transference; it is predominantly realistic, directed at problem solving to keep the patient from becoming too dependent or regressed. The major exception to this stance, however, is when the patient's response to the therapist is interfering with treatment, whereupon explicit attention is given to the relationship.

Aside from these general axioms, the therapeutic relationship can also be used as a specific means of addressing each of the major problem areas in depression. In the case of role disputes, direct feedback on how the depressed patient is perceived by others can be provided through similar interaction with the therapist and can then become a basis for communication and decision analysis. For a patient experiencing grief or loss, reactions to the therapist may mirror either the patient's relationship with the lost person or the manner in which he responds to other situations of interpersonal abandonment. In the case of social deficits, the relationship with the therapist becomes a model for the development of relationship skills.

The fundamental goals of the interpersonal approach relate to the need to maintain good interpersonal relations and social adaptability; they include reconstruction of present maladaptive relationships and, where possible, restoration of past losses. This means both coping with immediate stressful interactions and forming better or new relationships by developing problem-solving strategies and mastery in social skills. The therapist may also facilitate the mourning process for a patient who is actually or psychologically bereaved, then encourage him to find substitutes for the lost object and to use the loss as a means of growth. A more immediate goal, however, is the direct alleviation of depressive vegetative signs and symptoms, which acts as a preface to (and to some extent is independent of) the special interpersonal problem areas that are the heart of treatment.

Other interpersonal therapy tasks are minimizing dependency by helping the patient to better negotiate current relationships (including his relationship to the therapist) and maintain important roles vis-à-vis work, family, and peers, thereby improving self-esteem. While the interpersonal approach reduces dependency, an early educational aim is to facilitate the patient's acceptance of depression as a sanc-

TABLE 16–1. Major Features of Three Psychotherapeutic Approaches to Depression

Feature	Psychodynamic Approach	Cognitive Approach	Interpersonal Approach
Major theorists	Freud, Abraham, Jacobson, Kohut	Plato, Adler, Beck, Rush	Meyer, Sullivan, Klerman, Weissman
Concepts of pathology and etiology	Ego regression: damaged self-esteem and unresolved conflict due to childhood object loss and disappointment	Distorted thinking: dysphoria due to learned negative views of self, others, and the world	Impaired interpersonal relations: absent or unsatisfactory significant social bonds
Major goals and mechanisms of change	To promote personality change through understanding of past conflicts; to achieve insight into defenses, ego distortions, and superego defects; to provide a role model; to permit cathartic release of aggression	To provide symptomatic relief through alteration of target thoughts; to identify self-destructive cognitions; to modify specific erroneous assumptions; to promote self-control over thinking patterns	To provide symptomatic relief through solution of current interpersonal problems; to reduce stress involving family or work; to improve interpersonal communication skills
Primary techniques and practices	Expressive/empathic: fully or partially analyzing transference and resistance; confronting defenses; clarifying ego and superego distortions	Behavioral/cognitive: recording and monitoring cognitions; correcting distorted themes with logic and experimental testing; providing alternative thought content; homework	Communicative/environmental: clarifying and managing maladaptive relationships and learning new ones through communication and social skills training; providing information on illness

82

Therapist role/ therapeutic relationship	Interpreter/reflector: establishment and exploration of transference; therapeutic alliance for benign dependency and empathic understanding	Educator/shaper: psotive relationship instead of transference; collaborative empiricism as basis for joint scientific (logical) task	Explorer/prescriber: positive relationship/transference without interpretation; active therapist role for influence and advocacy
Marital/family role	Full individual confidentiality; exclusion of significant others except in life-threatening situations	Use of spouse as objective reporter; couples therapy for disturbed cognitions sustained in marital relationship	Integral role of spouse in treatment; examination of spouse's role in patient's predisposition to depression and impact of illness on marriage

tioned and real medical illness (5). In sum, according to the originators of interpersonal therapy, the goals of interpersonal therapy fall into two major categories—symptom formation and social and interpersonal relations (5).

Table 16–1 is a comparison of the major features of the three psychotherapeutic approaches to depression.

Part IV

ADVANTAGES AND LIMITATIONS OF THE THREE APPROACHES

17

Advantages and Limitations of the Psychodynamic Approach

Both advantages and disadvantages of each of the three psychotherapeutic approaches to depression are presented in Table 17-1.

Often the greatest contrast occurs when comparing the psychodynamic approach with the other two. This is in part because of the former's historical role in the development of the psychotherapies. Many forms of psychotherapy developed since Freud's time have addressed presumed failings of the psychoanalytic model; they are thus deliberate theoretical and/or technical departures from it, at least overtly (44). Placed in chronological perspective, for example, the analytic approach has the disadvantage of having originated as a general treatment of neuroses (chiefly characterized by anxiety) and was never designed for depressive disorders (33), whereas cognitive therapy and interpersonal therapy were specifically devised for depression (4, 5). In addition, although the analyst is an intentionally neutral and objective observer, the psychodynamic approach—which is based on the individual case study method, disguised (unconscious) data, and often open-ended time frame—has traditionally been the least amenable to standardization and research. This has limited attempts to replicate treatment and training and to

TABLE 17–1. Advantages and Limitations of Three Psychotherapeutic Approaches to Depression

Feature	Psychodynamic Approach	Cognitive Approach	Interpersonal Approach
Theory			
Advantages	Individual depth approach encourages patient to look inward for solutions rather than depending on external sources	Cognitive/behavioral orientation is tangible and objective	Interpersonal orientation addresses broader (e.g., social, family) context, useful in focusing on man-women relations
Limitations	Focus on intrapsychic phenomena may obscure other (e.g., interpersonal, environmental) factors; aggression = depression theory can be overgeneralized and lead to overreliance on catharsis	Cognitive/behavioral emphasis may neglect whole person, especially affective component; symptom-oriented perspective overlooks past history, complex problem areas, and hidden conflicts	Emphasis on four designated interpersonal problems can bias toward preconceived themes; interpersonal orientation may stress marital/family factors while underplaying intrapsychic forces
Goals			
Advantages	Enduring structural change transcends symptomatic relief; strengthened adaptive capacities can be useful beyond specific depressive pathology	Primary goals of symptom relief is expedient in itself and is first stage in changing cognitive style	Improvement of interpersonal relations is expedient in itself and may also result in relief of symptoms

Limitations	Personality alteration can be too ambitious and may be unnecessary or excessive for most depression diagnoses	Symptom reduction may be insufficient, superficial, or temporary; focus on current problems can preclude enduring modification of personality or prophylactic function of treatment	Symptom relief may be fragile and temporary if it is highly dependent on external factors
Structure			
Advantages	Indefinite duration allows long-term of flexible goals[a]	Brief or fixed duration is cost-effective and can foster results in short period, may heighten expectation of rapid change and encourage optimism	Predetermined duration is cost-effective; approach re-engages family and may have preventive effect
Limitations	Long-term or open-ended treatment is uneconomical and difficult to evaluate[a]	Short or predetermined duration may be insufficient or inflexible	Time limitation predetermines the extent of personal growth and independence
Therapist role			
Advantages	Neutral, accepting stance ensures nonjudgmental attitude and objectivity; receptive listening encourages transference formation and ensuing analytic process	Active therapist can directly intervene to interrupt depressive schemata and suggest alternatives to faulty thinking	Therapist position between activity and reactivity can reassure patient and provide supportive person for patient to relate to

(continued)

TABLE 17-1. (Continued)

Feature	Psychodynamic Approach	Cognitive Approach	Interpersonal Approach
Limitations	Transference regression can produce overidealization of therapist and underestimation of patient self-worth; therapist silence may be misconstrued as rejection, which can perpetuate depression and/or cause premature termination	Active suggestion and direction can undermine patient responsibility and self-esteem by imposing therapist point of view or values	Supportive interpersonal role may encourage dependency and rage at withdrawal of therapist
Techniques			
Advantages	Free association provides verbal catharsis; interpretations provide new understanding of depressogenic conflicts and historical events	Specific approach is directly tailored to depressed population and aims at particular target symptoms; identification of depressogenic assumptions and homework to test new thinking foster cognitive modification	Specific approach is directly tailored to depressed population and can address particular current interpersonal maladaptations
Limitations	No specific techniques developed; focus on past events and spontaneous associations may encourage repetitive litany of depressive complaints at the expense of present therapeutic tasks	Emphasis on specific cognitive schemata may bias toward certain preconceived themes; overt simplicity of techniques may lead to underestimation of technical skill required	Identification of specific interpersonal problem areas may be overly restrictive, yet techniques are relatively nonspecific; legitimation of patient sick role may encourage passivity

Research status			
Advantages	Longitudinal case study approach useful for detailed examination and follow-up of individual patients	Operational manual allows for replication of treatment and training and empirical establishment of efficacy	Same as for cognitive approach
Limitations	Idiographic approach or anecdotal case history is not amenable to controlled or comparative research	Research-oriented operationalized approach may become oversimplified formula for complex clinical phenomena	Same as for cognitive approach
Relation to other modalities			
Advantages	Integrity of transference is maintained through elimination of outside influences	Competition with pharmacotherapy encourages research on relative efficacy, especially instances when cognitive therapy alone is most effective	Approach designed to be used alone or with drugs; it is especially amenable to combination with marital therapy (manual is being developed for using conjoint marriage therapy as adjunct to individual treatment)

(continued)

TABLE 17–1. (Continued)

Feature	Psychodynamic Approach	Cognitive Approach	Interpersonal Approach
Limitations	Need for neutrality may limit use of other helpful treatment approaches (e.g., family therapy, drug treatment)	Competition with pharmacotherapy fosters polarization of approaches and partisan resistance to integration with drug treatment	Amenability to additive or eclectic modalities requires integrative theoretical model, clinical expertise in more than one modality, and/or ability to collaborate with other disciplines, which may lead to role diffusion and insufficient knowledge or training
Patient population Advantages	Special patient requisites (e.g., verbal orientation, psychological-mindedness) ensure maximal insight	Logical thinking ensures maximal potential to deal with and change depressogenic assumptions and thought patterns	Orientation toward interpersonal relations, especially marital interaction, can address gender issues in marriage, especially important given high prevalence of women among depressed patients

| Limitations | Special patient requisites may limit usefulness to verbal, psychological-minded population | Cognitively impaired population may not benefit; sophisticated, introspective patients may find approach too simple-minded or superficial | Interpersonal orientation may overemphasize marriage; primarily female population may bias toward women; conjoint focus may bias against unmarried population |

[a]Advantages/limitations of short-term psychodynamic therapy are similar to those for the cognitive and interpersonal approaches.

empirically establish efficacy (9, 77, 78). Moreover, its ambitious aim of modifying personality structure, sometimes within a relatively short period, may seem difficult in this day and age, especially with increased public pressure to demonstrate discernible effects in a short time.

With regard to both theory and techniques, the special problems of a psychodynamic approach to depression usually fall into three major categories: (a) overuse of catharsis, (b) pitfalls of a regressive transference and negative response to therapist silence, and (c) undue priority given to individual dynamics and the dyadic relationship as a closed system. Mendelson (43) has observed that equating depression with unconscious aggression in dynamic theory may foster overuse of the cathartic model. This formula may be fallacious both conceptually and clinically: theoretically, depression may be more of an ego than superego problem (a defect in self development, not simply an excess of aggressive cathexes), and technically it may be a mistake to focus on hostile feelings, especially early in treatment, since self-esteem must often be raised before anger can be usefully expressed, not the reverse.

With regard to transference, it has frequently been observed that the clinical manifestations of depression include persistent requests for magical relief and manipulative attempts by the patient to gain nurturance. Jacobson (29) has described the perils of allowing development of an unrealistic idealization of the therapist, to which patients in psychodynamic therapy are particularly prone. Although some degree of illusion is essential to the transferential process, and may even be therapeutic in the treatment of depressed borderline patients, it may unwittingly foster the very dynamics it tries to cure, i.e., excessive demands for love and gratification from an external source, if it is not worked through. Another danger of the analytic stance with depressed patients, who already have poor self-esteem, is the likelihood that therapist silence will be construed as rejection, leading to more depression and/or flight (11). In fact, Bemporad (42) recommended that the psychodynamic therapist not become a major focus of the patient's life and that, to break the monotonous litany of depressive complaints, the therapist needs to actively introduce new content, not remain reflective.

Finally, the traditional focus on the individual patient to the exclusion of outside contact may especially compromise treatment of depression, insofar as such patients are often unable to relinquish a premorbid relationship (e.g., with a spouse) that may predispose them to the illness. In such cases, it would be advisable to see the partners together or to arrange for family intervention (42). Forrest (79) stated that because of the reciprocal reinforcement of depression in marriage, it may be essential to see both parties, although such practices have traditionally been avoided in psychodynamic circles.

The total picture is balanced by the advantages of structural and technical aspects and the goals of the psychodynamic approach. For example, its introspective strategy encourages an inward search for solutions as an adaptive alternative to pathological reliance on external sources of esteem. The often open-ended orientation allows for a flexible response to patient needs and greater attention to the long-range future. Goals that transcend symptomatic relief can be useful beyond specific targeted problems, i.e., to strengthen general ego capacities and increase the prospects of permanent structural change. In addition, some of the flaws traditionally associated with psychodynamic therapy are being corrected by significant revisions in therapy format, strategy, and research (e.g., brief duration, combination of expressive and supportive techniques, development of standardized manuals) (6, 7).

18

Advantages and Limitations of the Cognitive and Interpersonal Approaches

A major advantage of cognitive therapy is that the therapist can directly intervene; it is used to interrupt thought patterns and actively help patients learn and practice logical alternatives. A fundamental asset of interpersonal therapy is that it addresses the broader social context of depressive risk and engages the family in treatment. Although both of these approaches are tailor-made for depression and offer obvious practical benefits, they are not without corresponding limitations. Highly focused aims may be too restricted, superficial, or temporary; emphasis on current problem areas or recent stresses can camouflage significant long-standing conflicts that need attention; a very directive approach may preempt patient initiative or discourage introspection; and a fixed-length or brief therapy can prematurely close off deeply concealed issues that take longer to emerge, allow less time for correcting diagnostic errors or overcoming resistances, or can even counteract treatment gains with a patient's disappointment about not achieving a more lasting cure. Moreover, the research need to operationalize treatment may foster reductionistic formulae that omit complex clinical phenomena or, more important, preclude the very nuances of individual technique and relationship that are crucial to personalized patient care.

Beyond the respective advantages and limitations of these particular approaches, all psychotherapies for depression may suffer from some of the same constraints, e.g., dedication to a particular point of view and resulting bias toward certain preferred themes or content areas. Examples are childhood conflicts, disappointment in parents, excessive guilt, and unexpressed rage (psychodynamic); marital disputes, environmental stresses, and gender or role problems (interpersonal); and preconceptions about self and future and illogical expectations of others (cognitive). The psychodynamic model may overemphasize unconscious processes and the primacy of affect (80), while cognitive therapy may overplay the role of thinking, and the interpersonal model may forgo the internal mechanisms of the disturbance for the socioenvironmental context in which it occurs.

The first major U.S. public health prevention program for a specific group of mental disorders—the NIMH Depression Awareness, Recognition, and Treatment Program—suggests that from 80% to 90% of persons with major depressive disorder can be treated successfully (81). This multi-institutional project is using the newly standardized cognitive and interpersonal therapies and in the near future will begin clinical trials with short-term dynamic psychotherapy. These efforts should include determination of for whom and when these treatment modalities are appropriate and whether they are most effective together or separately. Preliminary trials with imipramine for unipolar depression also suggest the need to specify the principles for combining the psychotherapies with other significant treatment modalities for depression, such as pharmacotherapy.

The systematic comparison of the three major psychotherapeutic approaches to depression today—cognitive, interpersonal, and dynamic—reveals that, as in the larger field of psychiatry, each school or treatment modality appears to be different from the others (at least overtly) in terms of its theoretical orientation, major goals, mechanisms of change, and techniques. At the same time, delineating these dimensions and the advantages and limitations of each approach sets the stage for revealing both the distinct and complementary features of the different approaches—what a particular modality offers to different types of patients and how one or more modalities have positive effects on all patients. Ultimately, this may pave the way for treating individual depressed patients in a highly selective fashion, drawing from the therapeutic elements of all available approaches and using them together and separately.

Part V

DEPRESSION AS A SPECTRUM PHENOMENON

19

The Range and Scope
of Depression

Depression spans the entire spectrum of pathology and health. It is manifested in an assortment of psychiatric disorders, which can be psychotic, neurotic, or characterological and can range in presentation from florid, biphasic mood shifts (82) to chronic mild malaise (83) or even masked symptoms that are disguised as behavioral disturbances (84). Depression is also a concomitant of abnormal and normal bereavement and of everyday oscillations of emotion.

Moreover, depressive episodes appear during all stages of the life cycle—as the "anaclitic" depression experienced by hospitalized infants in reaction to early maternal separation (85), as suicide and other behavioral expressions of underlying depression in adolescence (86), as a common concomitant of midlife (87), and as the progressive physiological deterioration that increasingly accentuates, but also sometimes conceals, functional depressive disorders in the aged (88). Each is associated with an advance from one major developmental phase to another, which inherently constitutes a psychological loss of past objects, experiences, and/or possibilities. This may in part account for the recent finding that age does not alter the basic phenomena of major depression, even though it differentially modifies the symptom profile in developmentally different populations. The core symptoms that remain unchanged with age are depressed mood, diminished ability to concentrate, sleep disturbance, and suicidal ideation (89).

In light of its ubiquity, depression has recently been classified into three global categories: normal emotion, symptom, and psychiatric disorder (90). At one end of the spectrum, depressed feelings or passing sadness may be regarded as a natural part of everyone's experience, as an adaptive response to everyday disappointments or as a universal reaction to the ontologic condition of all human existence in face of man's mortality (91). While some existential crises can precipitate a severe depression, most normal affective fluctuations are relatively benign, transient, appropriate to the situation, and reversible. At the other end of the spectrum is illness, the disorders involving "a prolonged emotion that colors the whole psychic life" (DSM-III-R, p. 213).

Studies of the similarities and differences between nonclinical depression and mourning have confirmed the resemblance between normal depression and uncomplicated bereavement (22). Beyond this, psychiatric depression has been succinctly defined as "a morbid sadness, dejection or melancholy" and is distinguished from nonmorbid "grief, which is realistic and proportionate to what has been lost" (92, p. 28). This overriding distinction, whose theoretic roots are found in Freud's classic "Mourning and Melancholia" (19), has both diagnostic and therapeutic implications. Pathological depression is both manifested and subjectively experienced as distinctly different from ordinary sadness (93) or a reaction to the real loss of a love object; it is frequently considered the consequence not of actual loss but of fantasized, excessive expectations that are not—indeed, by their very nature cannot be—fulfilled. Although they differ in duration and intensity, melancholia and mourning are both characterized by painful dejection, cessation of interest or pleasure in the outside world, inhibition of activity or motivation, diminution of the capacity to love, physical vegetative signs (such as reduced appetite or sleep disturbance), and even loss of the will to live or the active wish to die. However, what appears to significantly separate the two phenomena is the fundamental low self-regard in melancholia, which accounts for the profound self-denigration and self-approach that pervades the overall picture.

Other boundary problems relate to not only such fundamental distinctions as those between normal and morbid affective states, but also the differences between depression and anxiety, between affective and personality disorders, and between schizophrenia and affective psychoses (94). Other definitions also highlight the blurred boundaries in descriptions of depression. For example, depressed "affect" usually refers to transitory fluctuations in feelings, whereas depressed "mood" is frequently descriptive of more enduring emotional states (90). Such unresolved terminology is reflected in APA's *Diagnostic and Statistical Manual of Mental Disorders*, the first standardized diagnostic system to devote a separate category to affective disorders; the generic term "Affective Disorders" was changed to "Mood Disorders" when the manual was revised.

The clinical classification and diagnosis of depression is as yet unresolved (95). It has been a matter of concern and controversy since Kraepelin's pioneering designation of "manic-depressive insanity" nearly a century ago (96), which split major mental disorders of intense affect (either depression or elation) from those marked by the absence of affect, i.e., "dementia praecox" (later renamed "schizophrenia" by Bleuler [97]). Subsequent nosological systems (e.g., autonomous/reactive, endogenous/exogenous, bipolar/unipolar, psychotic/neurotic, primary/secondary, major/minor) have since reflected attempts to extend the affective realm to less severe forms of depression, often broadly differentiating chronic conditions (largely independent of the impact of external events) from situational varieties (related to acute or subacute environmental circumstances). In *DSM-III-R*, "Major Depression" is distinguished from "Dysthymia (or Depressive Neurosis)."

Even today there is still a tendency to dichotomize depressive disorder (98), but we do not yet know whether major depression and dysthymia are truly separate types of illness or exist on a clinical continuum. This question is an expression of the longstanding Kraepelinian/Meyerian dichotomy (binarian) versus continuity (unitarian) controversy (96). Its current status is reflected in a recent conclusion by Andreasen et al.: "Two different components are important in the classification of depression: severity and type of symptoms. The difference between subtypes is probably both qualitative and quantitative, both continuous and categorical. Although this conclusion is complex and paradoxical, it does reflect the reality of clinical practice" (99).

20

Implications for Treatment

The selection of therapy for an individual patient has typically been insufficient because the clinician bases the choice on (a) his own preferred modality and partisan conceptual position, irrespective of diagnosis, or (b) standardized diagnosis only, to the exclusion of other relevant variables. Both tendencies have begun to be subjected to criticism and reevaluation. Failure to recognize the range of treatments available and the possibility that another therapy may be more suitable than one's own has become a common theme in contemporary psychiatry (100–104). The tendency to address diagnosis only is the result of underappreciation of the spectrum of individual symptoms and patient profiles (105, 106).

The necessity for continual evaluation of standardized criteria for melancholia was pointed out by the originators of the concept themselves (97). In a recent reassessment of the unipolar-bipolar dichotomy, for example, it was proposed that the classification of depression incorporate such nonsymptom considerations as family history, temperament, abruptness of onset, periodicity and seasonality, and response to pharmacotherapy (107). Skodol and I (106) have presented the clinical profiles of three very different patients with dysthymic disorder who were nonetheless identical across all five *DSM-III* axes, and we suggested that there is a need for additional criteria for selection of treatment—e.g., goals of therapy, nature of explicit or implicit contract drawn, anticipated therapeutic relationship and its complications—to make it more individualized.

In sum, the present concept of depression as a spectrum of disorders is based on the complexity of definition and diagnosis and the increasing recognition that affective/mood disorders have many forms, according to their somatic, psychomotor, emotional, cognitive, and characterological features (94). Such a spectrum requires a flexible model of treatment in which particular aspects may be selected and/or integrated.

Part VI

PSYCHOTHERAPY AND PHARMACOTHERAPY: THREE APPROACHES

21

Psychodynamic Therapy Plus Pharmacotherapy

Conceptual or clinical resistance to pharmacotherapy by psychotherapists (and the resistance to psychotherapy by pharmacotherapists) has a long history and is a legacy of the post-Cartesian mind-body dichotomy that has always been at the core of modern medicine (108). The beginnings of an integrative model of psychotherapy and pharmacotherapy have appeared only recently. Affective disorders appear to be the most promising diagnoses with which to assess the additive effects of the two modalities combined (100). Each of the three major psychotherapeutic approaches to depression—psychodynamic, cognitive, and interpersonal—has its own strategies for using pharmacotherapy, which are based on its history and theoretical orientation toward conjoint treatment with medication.

Freud (109) anticipated the potential value of pharmacotherapy when he wrote, "The future may teach us to exercise a direct influence, by means of particular chemical substances. . . . It may be that there are other still undreamt of possibilities of therapy." Nonetheless, the fundamental clinical posture of psychoanalytic treatment has been based on the Freudian premise that symptoms of psychopathology (e.g., anxiety) are the patient's motivation for change and sustained

121

analytic work; reduction of symptoms by somatic means could thus destroy or reduce a crucial motivational source. Apart from this legacy (which may not be as applicable to depressed patients as it had been to anxious ones), psychoanalytic psychotherapists have traditionally resisted administration of pills because the tenets of classical technique inherently disparage methods that do not provoke insight, i.e., any form of external manipulation (110). The introduction of drugs has long been construed as an artifact that can confound the therapeutic transference (111).

Despite gradual modification of this view over the years (112), it is still believed that the major risk of administering pharmacologic agents during psychodynamic treatment is that the patient will use them as a crutch or substitute for introspection instead of relying on self-exploration (7). Luborsky (7) pointed out that psychodynamic progress may be impeded if the patient (a) considers taking medication an indication that he is giving up self-control and autonomy, (b) regards the recommendation to take pills as a sign that psychotherapy has failed, or (c) unrealistically views the therapist as an omnipotent figure because he administered the magical medication. (Although this does of course occur, to a greater or lesser degree, in any treatment, depressive patients are particularly vulnerable to over-endowing therapists and further diminishing their own self-esteem.) Other potential pharmacologic problems during expressive therapy have also been noted, such as the danger of misinterpreting drug side effects as psychological phenomena or the therapist's defensive resorting to drug administration at difficult points in exploratory work (113).

Although the combination of antidepressants and psychodynamic psychotherapy was rarely applied in the past, modern practice is much more flexible. The predominant psychodynamic stances and strategies regarding adjunctive treatment with pharmacotherapy include general avoidance of its use unless necessitated by an acute, life-threatening situation and, more recently, judicious titrating of pharmacologic agents, especially when somatic symptoms or vegetative signs are pronounced. When drugs are prescribed, their implications and personal meanings are to be explored and interpreted with the patient, as with any other events that are consciously or unconsciously brought into the psychodynamic treatment.

22

Cognitive Therapy Plus Pharmacotherapy

Overall, research results indicate cognitive therapy alone is effective with a substantial range of clinically depressed inpatients and outpatients and with nonpatients (college students with subclinical depression); the effects are equal to or greater than those of pharmacotherapy and are comparable to the effects of combined treatment (114–116). The results have been accompanied by recommendations for using pharmacotherapy in conjunction with cognitive therapy (4), since depression is heterogeneous and not all depressed patients respond to cognitive therapy alone.

Indications for combining it with pharmacotherapy include inadequate response to cognitive therapy, presence of severe somatic symptoms, impaired concentration and marked psychomotor difficulty, severe depression, history of mania, chronic maladaptive functioning with intermittent depression, evidence that a first-degree relative has responded to antidepressants, and ironically, poor compliance with a medical regimen. In addition, for some patients who do not seem to be responding to cognitive therapy, the conjoint application of antidepressants appears to break the impasse in therapy almost immediately (4).

Cognitive therapy methods specifically designed to increase adherence to medication regimens include written records of side effects and telephone calls to the patient to elicit and correct negative cognitions about medication. Cognitions that have been found to contribute to poor adherence to prescribed medication regimens fall into three categories: before medication (e.g., It's addicting; It's a sign of weakness to take it), during medication (e.g., I should feel good immediately), and general, which involve the depression itself and undermine the patient's willingness to take any medication (e.g., I am not ill; I am so ill that no treatment will help).

23

Interpersonal Therapy Plus Pharmacotherapy

Perhaps more than any other psychotherapeutic modality, interpersonal therapy has been shown to be effective in neurotic and acute depression when combined with drug treatment. In the major studies in this area (117–124), each modality had independent effects, as contrasted to synergistic effects, on different aspects of depressive illness. Pharmacotherapy improved sleep and other vegetative symptoms, whereas interpersonal therapy altered such psychological symptoms as apathy and hopelessness. At 1-year follow-up, combined treatment again proved superior to either alone. In addition, different response latencies were observed: drug effects occurred early in treatment, often within the first week, whereas psychotherapy effects occurred later (118).

Klerman et al. described the combination of interpersonal therapy and pharmacotherapy in depression as a selective but accepted aspect of interpersonal therapy (5). They contended that generally the problems of combined psychotherapy and pharmacotherapy treatment are more attitudinal than real; that is, they do not lie in understanding (or misunderstanding) the pharmacology of drugs or specific problems of treatment but, instead, involve patient and/or therapist views reflecting either larger social values about medication or individual

TABLE 23–1. Approach to Pharmacotherapy of Three Psychotherapies for Depression

Feature of Combined Treatment	Psychodynamic Therapy	Cognitive Therapy	Interpersonal Therapy
Basic stance	Medication is avoided except in life-threatening situation, used judiciously for severe vegetative signs	Pharmacotherapy and cognitive therapy alone are in ongoing competition, but drugs are used in case of poor response to cognitive therapy and for breaking psychotherapeutic impasses in severe depression when symptomatic relief is required	Interpersonal therapy and pharmacotherapy are considered having different effects and response timetables (early drug effects on vegetative symptoms, later psychotherapy effects on suicidal ideation, work, and interests)
Techniques	Personal (unconscious and/or conscious) meanings are explored and interpreted within therapy session	Information and rationale for use is provided; special tasks are assigned to increase adherence, e.g., postsession homework (lists of side effects); phone contact with therapist is encouraged	Information and rationale for use is provided, in line with medical model; time is set aside in each session to discuss pharmacological issues

feelings about its use. Rounsaville et al. (122), using clinical data from another study (121), expressly disconfirmed six major hypotheses regarding negative aspects of the psychotherapy-pharmacotherapy interaction.

In earlier research (123) it was found that higher scores on a neuroticism scale were correlated with chronic poor response to one or both treatments up to 4 years after the acute episode. In examining diagnostic subtypes of depression as predictors of differential response to interpersonal therapy and/or drug treatment, Prusoff et al. (124) found that both nonendogenous and endogenous depression responded to combined treatment, the latter did not respond to interpersonal therapy alone, and the former responded to either alone, suggesting that it may be unnecessary to use combined treatment for situational depression.

Klerman et al.'s technical suggestions included giving the patient a preliminary explanation of the rationale for each intervention. During treatment itself they advocated setting aside a specific time, usually at the beginning of each session, to discuss pharmacotherapy therapy issues (e.g., side effects). Another major technical issue for interpersonal therapists is whether there will be one or two therapists for combined treatment; cooperation between psychotherapist and pharmacotherapist is needed when treatment is split.

Table 23–1 compares the three types of psychotherapy for depression with regard to their respective clinical stances and specific techniques.

Part VII

PSYCHOTHERAPY AND PHARMACOTHERAPY: A SELECTIVE AND INTEGRATIVE APPROACH

24

Complementary Roles

Although controlled efficacy studies suggest that over 60% of depressed patients improve with common tricyclic drugs (125), the other side of the coin is that nearly 40% do not. Other real constraints of pharmacotherapy in affective illness are the relatively high relapse rate of depressed patients treated with medication (nearly one-half in the year immediately after termination of treatment) and the failure to prevent suicide with antidepressant drug treatment, even after having averted a suicidal crisis (126). From the drug-responsive group may also be subtracted those who show significant side effects (127).

These outcomes can occur with or without the adverse psychological impact of irrational fears or myths about medication (112), which can themselves confound the pharmacologic response. For example, a variety of undesirable psychological concomitants of pharmacology have been cited in the treatment literature, including fear of functioning without external aids and loss of the patient's sense of autonomy as chemicals become a crutch and discourage other, self-initiated therapeutic efforts (128, 129). This possibility is particularly salient with depressed patients, whose reliance on chemotherapy may unwittingly undermine their easily diminished egos and deplete already limited inner resources for coping with depression (4). Still other depressed patients, albeit potentially responsive, may unconsciously or consciously reject medication for subjective (personal, religious, cultural) reasons. In fact, although there are many explanations for nonresponse to drugs, noncompliance with the medical regimen is an often neglected contributor (130); surveys indicate 25% to 50% of those treated for affective illness fail to take their medication as prescribed, reducing or discontinuing its use (131).

On the other hand, however, many patients lack access to psychotherapeutic intervention, and unlike anxiety, depression inherently retards psychomotor energy and motivation for change. In addition, marked resistance at any point during the therapeutic interaction (29) can be exacerbated by the depressed patient's vulnerability to narcissistic injury and by consequent countertherapeutic interpersonal maneuvers to compensate for object loss within the therapist-patient relationship.

These factors illustrate the complementary roles of drugs and psychotherapy; drugs can facilitate a patient's receptivity to psychological intervention by controlling episodes of irritability or apathy, which produce impasses in the interaction between patient and therapist, while psychotherapy may be used for increasing compliance with medication regimens. In fact, specific techniques for drug compliance have been directly incorporated into both cognitive and interpersonal therapy for depressed patients (4, 5). The extension of psychotherapeutic approaches to the patient's spouse or family can also help neutralize the negative influence of family members who otherwise sabotage efforts to adhere to a medication schedule. A major role of psychotherapy may thus be to enhance the response to chemotherapy, by inducing patients to remain in treatment for longer periods, or to provide alternative long-term care for those who do not obtain full prophylaxis or remission from antidepressant medication.

25

Indications

The following clinical model is based on the finding that psychotherapy is increasingly being shown to be effective in the treatment of major depression, alone or in combination with pharmacotherapy (9, 100, 132, 133), and it begins where my earlier combined treatment model for depression left off (100). The prior model was based on the finding that the two treatments together are superior to either intervention by itself: (a) the two modalities have different effects—drugs primarily affect symptom formation and affective distress, whereas psychotherapy more directly influences interpersonal relations and social adjustment, (b) the two are activated and sustained at different times—drugs may take effect sooner and last for shorter periods, whereas psychotherapy results may not reveal themselves until later but can last longer, and (c) they may work best with different diagnoses and subtypes—drugs with time-limited and autonomous state disorders, psychotherapy with more enduring trait disorders (100). In brief, although research on combined treatment has special problems, it seems to indicate that the two modalities are independent and complementary in terms of active ingredients, mechanisms of change, and latency of response (77, 78, 114, 120, 134).

TABLE 25–1. Indications for Psychotherapy and Pharmacotherapy in the Treatment of Depression

Variable	Indications for Treatment[a]	
	Pharmacotherapy	Psychotherapy
DSM-III-R symptom criteria for major depression		
Depressed mood	Marked vegetative signs; extreme or uncontrolled mood	Mild to moderate situational or characterological depressed mood
Diminished interest or pleasure	Anhedonia; loss of libido; impaired sexual function or performance	Apathy, decreased enjoyment; diminished sexual desire or gratification
Weight loss or gain	Significant weight loss	Insignificant weight gain
Insomnia or hypersomnia	Early morning wakening	Oversleeping, morbid dreams or nightmares
Psychomotor agitation	Hyperactivity or motor retardation	Restlessness or feelings of being slowed down
Fatigue or loss of energy (anergia)	Depressive stupor	Lack of motivation or will
Feelings of worthlessness or excessive guilt	Nihilistic or self-deprecatory delusions, self-berating auditory hallucinations	Low self-esteem, inappropriate guilt feelings, self-reproach
Diminished ability to think or concentrate, indecisiveness	Loss of control over thinking, obsessive rumination, inability to focus or act	Distractibility, sluggish thinking or decision making; negative cognitions
Recurrent thoughts of death or suicide	Acute, episodic, and uncontrolled suicidal acts or plans[b]	Chronic feelings of hopelessness or helplessness[c]

144

Associated features	Panic (anxiety) attacks or phobias; persecutory delusions; pseudodementia; physical symptoms or somatic delusions	Social withdrawal or fears of rejection or failure; psychosomatic complaints or hypochondriasis
Family history	Genetic loading (bipolar or unipolar illness)	No genetic loading (dysthymia)
Predisposing factors	Other mental disorders, e.g., schizophrenia, alcoholism, anorexia nervosa	Psychosocial stressors, e.g., loss of significant other, change in status or role
Personality disorders	Borderline, histrionic, obsessive-compulsive	Dependent, inadequate, masochistic

[a]These are not mutually exclusive categories.
[b]Hospitalization may be required.
[c]Medication may also be useful.

In my earlier model of combined therapy for affective disorders (100), pharmacotherapy was considered the better treatment for mania and major, endogenous depression, whereas psychotherapy was thought to be preferable for minor, reactive, or nonendogenous disorders. However, the diagnostic changes reflected in *DSM-III* in part mirror the new thinking in clinical practice that pharmacotherapy need not be limited to the most severe types of affective disorder (135) and, the converse, that psychotherapy need no longer be relegated to mild forms of depression only (136). Table 25–1 presents a model of combined psychotherapy-pharmaco-therapy that goes beyond the diagnostic rubric in two ways: to the spectrum of signs and symptoms of affective disorders and to clinical variables other than the standard diagnostic boundaries. The constraints of the model must also be noted: these variables are not intended to be all-inclusive and have not been subjected to rigorous research and clinical trials. Moreover, the division of variables between pharmacotherapy and psychotherapy is not meant to imply they are categorical or mutually exclusive but, rather, provides a framework for their selective application within an additive treatment model.

This clinical model emerges out of, and therefore does not negate, the most updated standardized diagnostic guidelines for depression; it breaks diagnosis down to quantitative and qualitative variables that may each respond to either pharmacotherapy or psychotherapy. Major depression is initially broken down into the nine symptom-related criteria designated in *DSM-III-R* (see Table 25–1).

This model suggests that the symptoms of depression have many dimensions: physiological (hypersomnolence, weight loss, somatic disorders, psychomotor retardation), affective (depressed mood, guilt, repressed anger, anxiety), cognitive (negative, pessimistic perceptions and ruminations), interpersonal (social withdrawal, increased helplessness), and behavioral (reduced activities, increased dependency, self-destructive acts) (5). Some of these manifestations are better treated with pharmacotherapy, others with psychotherapy. For example, while psychotic thinking, especially persecutory or nihilistic delusions and auditory hallucinations, can be appropriately treated with medication, persistent irrational beliefs that reflect negative distortion or exaggeration but not psychosis can be effectively treated with psychotherapy. Such differential treatment also applies to observable psychomotor agitation or retardation versus feelings of restlessness or being slowed down and early morning wakening versus morbid dreams or nightmares.

These symptoms, signs, and associated features may not suffice, either quantitatively or qualitatively, as clinical criteria in developing a combined psychotherapy-pharmacotherapy model. The contributions of a variety of other relevant variables, e.g., family history, nature of onset, predisposing factors, and personality type, pose the need for vigorous research and eventually a more comprehensive joint treatment model of depression that takes diverse genetic (137), environmental (138), physiological (139), and biochemical (140, 141) factors into account (1).

Part VIII

SELECTING PSYCHOTHERAPY FOR INDIVIDUALIZED TREATMENT

26

Different Treatments and Different Effects

In addition to the aforementioned variables are the therapeutic vicissitudes of the treatments themselves, the patients for whom they are best suited, their processes, and their goals. Not only may patients be differentially amenable to different treatment modalities, but different treatments may produce different effects.

Table 26–1 sets the stage for using the three models of the treatment of depression as both unique and potentially complementary. It first lists some "nonselective" variables—hyperphagia, hypersomnolence, leaden feeling, sensitivity to rejection, feelings of inadequacy, diminished self-esteem and interest, anergia, undue guilt, difficulty in concentration or decision making, recurrent thoughts of death, unrealistic ego ideals and expectations, helplessness, hopelessness, and deficits in interpersonal relations—that may be shared, to greater or lesser degrees, by all depressed patients and may be helped by any of the three psychotherapies or by other approaches not discussed here. It then lists an additional array of "selective" variables that may call for or contraindicate each of the three specific psychotherapeutic approaches. These variables include not only DSM-III-R diagnostic features and other individual variables, but the goals and overall

TABLE 26–1. Nonselective and Selective Patient Variables for Psychotherapy of Depression

Nonselective Patient Variables	Selective Patient Variables		
	Psychodynamic Therapy	Cognitive Therapy	Interpersonal Therapy
Feelings of hopelessness and helplessness	Chronic sense of emptiness and underestimation of self-worth	Obvious distorted thoughts about self, world, and future	Recent, focused dispute with spouse or significant other
Apathy, decreased enjoyment, diminished desire or gratification	Loss or long separation in childhood	Pragmatic (logical) thinking	Social or communication problems
Too high ego ideals and expectations	Conflicts in past relationships (e.g., with parent, sexual partner)	Real inadequacies (including poor response to other psychotherapies)	Recent role transition or life change
Oversleeping, morbid dreams or nightmares	Capacity for insight	Moderate to high need for direction and guidance	Abnormal grief reaction
Feelings of restlessness or being slowed down	Ability to modulate regression	Responsiveness to behavioral training and self-help (high degree of self-control)	Modest to moderate need for direction and guidance
Lack of motivation or will	Access to dreams and fantasy		Responsiveness to environmental manipulation (available support network)
Low self-esteem, inappropriate or excessive guilt and self-reproach	Little need for direction and guidance		
Distractibility, sluggish thinking or decision making	Stable environment		
Wish or intention to be dead			
Social withdrawal, fear of rejection or failure			
Psychosomatic complaints, hypochondriasis			

characteristics of each approach—in short, a blend of patient and technical psychotherapeutic factors that can be used in selecting one or more modalities for individualized treatment.

27

Patient Variables
for Different Approaches

The goals of the psychodynamic approach are insight, conflict resolution, and personality modification, and its methods are examination of the intrapsychic structure of illness, in-depth exploration, and longitudinal, developmental orientation to the present in relation to the past. It may be particularly suitable for treating chronic, pervasive low self-esteem and dejection and excessive feelings of guilt, especially in patients with severe real losses, extended separation in childhood, or long-standing unresolved conflicts related to attachment and loss in early relationships. At the same time, the psychodynamic approach generally requires that patients have a capacity for trust, good object relations, and a relatively stable environment and social support system. They must also be psychologically minded, have the capacity for insight and self-understanding, and have the ego strength to modulate regression when frustrated by a relatively neutral therapist within a transferential relationship. When the therapist is more direct or active (in short-term psychodynamic approaches), the patient must especially be able to deal with the anxiety resulting from confrontation of his defenses, early presentation of his conflicts, or immediate focus on the transference. These requisites, of course, are moderated by the duration, flexibility, and focus of the particular psychodynamic treatment and whether an open-ended (3), short-term (6, 7, 39, 142), or set time frame (37) is used.

Whereas the psychodynamic approach primarily focuses on the internal mechanisms of the illness, individual memory, and childhood antecedents of current object relations and achieves its goals through confrontation or interpretation of defenses and the patient's gradual uncovering of unconscious motivations, the interpersonal approach mainly addresses the social context or consequences of the illness, focuses on current environmental stressors and life events, emphasizes the recognition of assets, helps the patient correct misinformation, and provides direct advice on alternatives. It may be especially helpful for patients with recent, focused interpersonal disputes or communication problems, for those who are acutely distressed over a major role transition or marital discord, and those who have experienced real losses. Gotlib and Asarnow (143) found that depressed subjects performed significantly more poorly on an interpersonal problem-solving task than on an impersonal task. This was interpreted as evidence for the specificity of an interpersonal problem-solving deficit in depressed individuals. Discernible interpersonal problems or social deficits could also be subjected to environmental manipulation (e.g., a marital partner brought into treatment). Interpersonal therapy's communication/environmental methods (i.e., clarification and management of maladaptive relationships and negotiation of new ones through communication and social skills training) may be especially useful with depressed patients who need more active engagement with the therapist. These patients may also rely more on outside relations for self-esteem and productive functioning than patients who are appropriate for a psychodynamic approach.

The cognitive approach would be most suited to patients whose negative distortions of themselves, the world, and/or the future are readily apparent. In validating its unique effects, for example, Rush et al. (144) found that cognitive therapy had a more pervasive and significant impact on self-concept by the end of treatment than did amitriptyline, and it also resulted in quicker reduction of hopelessness. These findings suggest that this type of approach specifically improves patients' views of themselves. Patients with greater cognitive distortions responded better to cognitive therapy than did patients with less negative thinking.

The methods of cognitive/behavioral therapy do not require that the recipients of cognitive therapy be introspective. Rather, they can be pragmatic and therefore capable and responsive to logical thinking that does not demand a capacity for insight. They may also be more in need of strong guidance and direction for developing new patterns of thought. Such patients have been shown to have a high capacity for self-control (145), so they may especially benefit from behavioral exercises and home practice, which are an integral part of cognitive therapy.

Part IX

CONCLUSIONS

28

No Uniformly Successful
Single Therapy

The variation of depression in terms of etiology, manifestations, and response to treatment is well documented (82, 94, 146). Moreover, no single therapy is uniformly successful for all the concomitants of the depressive disorder (117, 118). For instance, biological variables may override psychological ones, or the reverse. In addition to determining whether treatment should consist of drugs combined with psychotherapy or of psychotherapy alone, examination of the three psychotherapies lends itself to a more discriminatory use of each, as indicated in Parts I–IV of this book.

Psychotherapy may be effective alone or combined with pharmacotherapy for a variety of patients and variables pertaining to both the illness itself and to change mechanisms and timing of treatment effects (77, 78). In some instances, a distorted viewpoint that has been targeted for change is isolated, recorded, monitored, logically analyzed, and ultimately brought under the patient's control with the teaching and support of the therapist. This process brings about salutary change, overt symptom relief, and/or prophylactic effects that endure beyond the acute episode and can be applied to subsequent recurrences. In other cases, the sociocultural context may be crucial because of specific environmental stressors. In yet other cases, where the effects of these approaches are at best temporary and changes in depressogenic thinking or environmental management do not alter chronic conflicts or profound fears of loss of love, a deeper approach may be necessary to tap the unconscious memories or schemata beneath the surface, thereby requiring greater efforts toward structural modification.

Psychotherapy may thus be used not only by default, that is, to increase compliance with medication or as an alternative for patients who cannot or will not respond to pharmacotherapy, but in itself as an independent intervention. Cognitive therapy can be used to change depressogenic attitudes and ingrained thinking patterns. Interpersonal therapy emphasizes teaching specific communication and social skills to counteract deficits or disputes involving a spouse or significant others in one's personal or work life; these deficits can be causes or consequences of depression. Psychodynamic therapy addresses the individual's intrapsychic conflictual personality structure so that the underlying demoralization of the damaged self, which dominates the clinical core of depression, can be understood and thus altered.

Although these three psychotherapeutic approaches represent different conceptualizations of depression as a disorder and have direct implications for therapeutic processes and change agents, even in the operationalized, research-oriented manuals they are not represented as categorical in practice (4–7). They have the common elements shared by all psychotherapies (e.g., benign human relationship) (147, 148), and they may complement each other in their basic modus operandi and in fundamental change agents, i.e., cognitive mastery, affective experiencing, and behavioral regulation (102, 104). Moreover, the controversy of non-specificity versus specificity of therapeutic effects (104) might be resolved by acknowledging that the former sets the stage for the latter. Common elements (empathy, positive regard) are applied to establish contact with the patient (therapeutic alliance), while specific techniques can be applied separately or together to bring about affective, cognitive, and/or behavioral changes. Simultaneously, each modality may be highly specific—applicable to certain subgroups of depressed individuals. The prototypical depressed patient in interpersonal therapy has recent, focused disputes with a spouse or significant other, cognitive therapy patients are characterized by habitual faulty thinking, and dynamic therapy is suited for patients with chronic conflict and lack of self-esteem. These and other psychotherapeutic approaches must also interact with pharmacological treatment, which has its own variations in efficacy and specificity (9, 77, 78).

29

Shifting and Sharing
Therapeutic Perspectives

Future directions for research thus entail increasing refinement of depressive subtypes, both diagnostically and therapeutically. In terms of diagnosis, we must identify depressed patients' particular assortment of symptoms, severity and level of functional impairment (149), and their accompanying biological, psychological, and social characteristics. In terms of therapy, we must determine doses and durations of treatment, identify effective combinations, and determine sequences of response. However, neither search need preclude addressing what all depressed patients or all therapies for depression hold in common. The proposed approach to clinical practice is therefore both integrative and selective. The integrative aspect pertains to collective qualities of all patients and to shared aspects of different therapeutic approaches, in whole or in part. The selective aspect refers to special features of such patients and therapies—what they can contribute together and separately.

Recognizing depression as a spectrum phenomenon is the first step. The diagnosis of unipolar depression, for example, may not define a population narrowly enough to permit proper patient assessment or determination of effective techniques for these particular patients. The diagnostic task of the future is thus to identify biopsychosocial variables that go beyond symptoms alone in delineating the individual clinical disposition. There is also a parallel need for recognition of increasing diversity in the treatment armamentarium for depressive disorders, both within the psychotherapeutic domain (e.g., cognitive, interpersonal, psychodynamic, and other therapies) and outside its boundaries (e.g., pharmacotherapy). Achievement of maximal therapeutic efficacy necessitates not simply knowledge of one's own school or theoretical orientation but appreciation of what other modalities and techniques have to offer (149, 150). In the best of all worlds, psychiatrists may well master only one modality, with which they identify and maintain allegiance, yet be well versed in the wide spectrum of strategies available. Moreover, both psychiatrists and primary care physicians can bear in mind an unanticipated, newly published finding from the National Institute of Mental Health Treatment of Depression Collaborative Research Program (149): the value in the clinical management of depressed patients of an initial supportive approach (sympathetic attention and encouragement beyond pill placebo), with or without pharmacotherapy—before specific treatment begins (151).

In sum, instead of focusing on which single school of therapy is effective for the large universe of unipolar depression, ideally one should take a highly individualized approach to meet each depressed individual's needs, using a broad-based but selective shifting and sharing of therapeutic perspectives. Realization of this effort, however, may be reminiscent of sentiments expressed over three centuries ago in *Anatomy of Melancholy*, the first detailed description of depression and its treatment. Its author, English clergyman and scholar Robert Burton, who suffered from chronic depression himself, despairingly suggested that "for this particular disease, him that shall take upon him to cure it . . . will have to be a Magician, a Chemist, a Philosopher, an Astrologer"

(152 p. 390). The therapy of depression may no longer be as difficult a task as it was in Burton's day, but as an early portent of the need for an approach to depressive disorders that is both integrative and selective, his multifaceted model still holds.

References

1. Flach FF, Draghi SC. *The Nature and Treatment of Depression*. New York: John Wiley & Sons, 1975.
2. Lieberman M. *Survey and Evaluation of the Literature on Verbal Psychotherapy of Depressive Disorders*. Rockville, Md: National Institute of Mental Health, Clinical Research Branch, March 7, 1975.
3. Arieti S, Bemporad J. *Severe and Mild Depression*. New York: Basic Books, 1978.
4. Beck AT, Rush AH, Shaw BF, et al. *Cognitive Therapy of Depression*. New York: Guilford Press, 1979.
5. Klerman GL, Weissman MM, Rounsaville BJ, et al. *Interpersonal Psychotherapy of Depression*. New York: Basic Books, 1984.
6. Strupp HH, Binder JL. *Psychotherapy in a New Key: A Guide to Time-Limited Dynamic Psychotherapy*. New York: Basic Books, 1984.
7. Luborsky L. *Principles of Psychoanalytic Psychotherapy: A Manual for Supportive-Expressive Treatment*. New York: Basic Books, 1984.
8. Jarrett RB, Rush AJ. Psychotherapeutic approaches for depression. In *Psychiatry*, vol 1, edited by Cavenar JO Jr, Michels R, Brodie HKH, et al. Philadelphia: JB Lippincott, and New York, Basic Books, 1985.

9. Conte H, Plutchik R, Wild K, et al. Combined psychotherapy and pharmacotherapy for depression: a systematic analysis of the evidence. *Arch Gen Psychiatry* 1986;43:471–479.

10. Kovacs M. Psychotherapies for depression. In *Psychiatry Update: The American Psychiatric Association Annual Review*, vol 2, edited by Grinspoon L. Washington, DC: American Psychiatric Press, 1983.

11. Altschuler KZ, Rush AJ. Psychoanalytic and cognitive therapies: a comparison of theories and tactics. *Am J Psychother* 1984;38:4–15.

12. Rush AJ (ed). *Short-Term Psychotherapies for Depression*. New York: Guilford Press, 1982.

13. Hole RW Jr. Psychotherapies or psychotherapy? *Contemporary Psychiatry* 1983;2:41–43.

14. Freud S. Three essays on the theory of sexuality (1905). In *Complete Psychological Works*, standard ed, vol 7. London: Hogarth Press, 1953.

15. Abraham K. Notes on the psycho-analytic investigation and treatment of manic-depressive insanity and allied conditions (1911). In *Selected Papers on Psycho-Analysis*. London: Hogarth Press and Institute of Psycho-Analysis, 1927.

16. Freud S. Notes upon a case of obsessional neurosis (1909). In *Complete Psychological Works*, standard ed, vol 10. London: Hogarth Press, 1955.

17. Abraham K. The first pregenital stage of the libido (1916). In *Selected Papers on Psycho-Analysis*. London: Hogarth Press and Institute of Psycho-Analysis, 1927.

18. Freud S. On narcissism: an introduction (1914). In *Complete Psychological Works*, standard ed, vol 14. London: Hogarth Press, 1957.

19. Freud S. Mourning and melancholia (1917[1915]). In *Complete Psychological Works*, standard ed, vol 14. London: Hogarth Press, 1957.

20. Abraham K. A short study of the development of the libido, viewed in the light of mental disorders (1924). In *Selected Papers on Psycho-Analysis*. London: Hogarth Press and Institute of Psycho-Analysis, 1927.

21. Lindemann E. Symptomatology and management of acute grief. *Am J. Psychiatry* 1944;101:141–148.
22. Clayton P, Desmarais L, Winokur G. A study of normal bereavement. *Am J Psychiatry* 1968;125:168–178.
23. Clayton PJ, Herjanic M, Murphy GE, et al. Mourning and depression: their similarities and differences. *Can J Psychiatry* 1974;19:309–312.
24. Rado S. The problem of melancholia. *Int J Psychoanal* 1928;9:420–438.
25. Klein M. A contribution to the psychogenesis of manic-depressive states (1934). In *Contributions to Psycho-Analysis, 1921–1945.* London: Hogarth Press and Institute of Psycho-Analysis, 1948.
26. Fenichel O. *The Psychoanalytic Theory of Neurosis.* New York: WW Norton, 1945.
27. Bibring E. The mechanism of depression. In *Affective Disorders,* edited by Greenacre P. New York: International Universities Press, 1953.
28. Sandler J, Joffee WG. Notes on childhood depression. *Int J Psychoanal* 1965;46:88–96.
29. Jacobson E. *Depression.* New York: International Universities Press, 1971.
30. Kohut H. *The Analysis of the Self.* New York: International Universities Press, 1971.
31. Kohut H. *The Restoration of the Self.* New York: International Universities Press, 1977.
32. Arieti S. Psychotherapy of severe depression. *Am J Psychiatry* 1977;134:864–868.
33. Strupp HH, Sandell JA, Waterhouse GJ, et al. Psychodynamic therapy: theory and research. In *Short-Term Psychotherapies for Depression,* edited by Rush AJ. New York: Guilford Press, 1982.
34. Zaiden J. Psychodynamic therapy: clinical applications. In *Short-Term Psychotherapies for Depression,* edited by Rush AJ. New York: Guilford Press, 1982.
35. Greenson R. *The Technique and Practice of Psychoanalysis,* vol 1. New York: International Universities Press, 1967.

36. Sifneos P. *Short-Term Psychotherapy and Emotional Crisis.* Cambridge, Mass: Harvard University Press, 1972.

37. Mann J. *Time-Limited Psychotherapy.* Cambridge, Mass: Harvard University Press, 1973.

38. Davanloo H (ed). *Basic Principles and Techniques in Short-Term Dynamic Psychotherapy.* New York: SP Medical & Scientific Books, 1978.

39. Malan D. *The Frontier of Brief Psychotherapy.* New York: Plenum, 1976.

40. Gill M. Psychoanalysis and psychotherapy: a revision. *Int Rev Psychoanal* 1984;11:161–179.

41. Karasu TB. Psychoanalysis and psychoanalytic psychotherapy. In *Comprehensive Textbook of Psychiatry*, 5th ed, vol 2, edited by Kaplan HI, Sadock BJ. Baltimore: Williams & Wilkins, 1989.

42. Bemporad J. Change factors in the treatment of depression. In *Curative Factors in Dynamic Psychotherapy*, edited by Slipp S. New York: McGraw-Hill, 1982.

43. Mendelson M. *Psychoanalytic Concepts of Depression.* New York: Spectrum Publications, 1974.

44. Karasu TB. Psychotherapies: an overview. *Am J Psychiatry* 1977;134:851–863.

45. Freud S. The unconscious (1915). In *Complete Psychological Works, standard ed*, vol 14. London: Hogarth Press, 1957.

46. Volkan VD. Identification and related psychic events. In *Curative Factors in Dynamic Psychotherapy*, edited by Slipp S. New York: McGraw-Hill, 1982.

47. Adler A. *What Life Should Mean To You* (1931). New York: Capricorn, 1958.

48. Karasu TB. Recent developments in individual psychotherapy. *Hosp Community Psychiatry* 1984;35:29–39.

49. Kelly G. *The Psychology of Personal Constructs*, vols 1, 2. New York: WW Norton, 1955.

50. Ellis A. *Reason and Emotion in Psychotherapy.* New York: Lyle Stuart, 1962.

51. Beck AT, Hurvich MS. Psychological correlates of depression, I: frequency of "masochistic" dream content in a private

practice sample. *Psychosom Med* 1959;21:50–55.

52. Kovacs M, Beck AT. Maladaptive cognitive structures in depression. *Am J Psychiatry* 1978;135:525–533.

53. Beck AT, Greenberg RL. *Coping With Depression*. New York: Institute for Rational Living, 1974.

54. Young JE, Beck AT. Cognitive therapy: clinical applications. In *Short-Term Psychotherapies for Depression*, edited by Rush AJ. New York: Guilford Press, 1982.

55. Meyer A. *Psychobiology: A Science of Man*. Springfield, Ill: Charles C Thomas, 1957.

56. Darwin C. *The Expression of Emotions in Man and Animals*. London: John Murray, 1872.

57. Sullivan HS. *The Interpersonal Theory of Psychiatry*. New York: WW Norton, 1953.

58. Bowlby J. *Attachment*. New York: Basic Books, 1969.

59. Bowlby J. The making and breaking of affectional bonds, II: some principles of psychotherapy. *Br J Psychiatry* 1977; 130:421–431.

60. Rutter M. *Maternal Deprivation Reassessed*. London: Penguin Books, 1972.

61. Paykel ES, Myers JK, Dienelt MN, et al. Life events and depression: a controlled study. *Arch Gen Psychiatry* 1969;21:753–760.

62. Klerman G. The psychobiology of affective states: the legacy of Adolf Meyer. In *Psychobiology of Human Behavior*, edited by Brady J, Meyer E. Baltimore: Johns Hopkins University Press, 1979.

63. Brown GW, Harris T, Copeland JR. Depression and loss. *Br J Psychiatry* 1977;130:1–18.

64. Weissman MM, Paykel ES. *The Depressed Woman: A Study of Social Relationships*. Chicago: University of Chicago Press, 1974.

65. Harlow HF, Harlow MK, Suomi SJ. From thought to therapy: lessons from a primate laboratory. *Am Scientist* 1971; 59:538–549.

66. Henderson S. A development in social psychiatry: the systematic study of social bonds. *J Nerv Ment Dis* 1981;168:63–69.

67. Henderson S, Byrne DG, Duncan P. *Neurosis and the Social Environment.* San Diego: Academic Press, 1982.

68. Miller P, Ingham JG. Friends, confidants and symptoms. *Soc Psychiatry* 1976;11:51–58.

69. Roy A. Vulnerability factors and depression in women. *Br J Psychiatry* 1978;133:106–110.

70. Holmes TH, Rahe RH. The Social Readjustment Rating Scale. *J Psychosom Res* 1967;11:213–218.

71. Paykel E. Recent life events in the development of depressive disorders. In *The Psychobiology of Depressive Disorders: Implications for the Effects of Stress,* edited by Defue EA. New York: Academic Press, 1978.

72. Hinchliffe MK, Hooper D, Roberts FJ. *The Melancholy Marriage.* New York: John Wiley & Sons, 1978.

73. Rounsaville BJ, Prusoff BA, Weissman MM. The course of marital disputes in depressed women: a 48-month follow-up study. *Compr Psychiatry* 1980;21:111–118.

74. Orvaschel H, Weissman MM, Kidd KK. Children and depression—the children of depressed parents; the childhood of depressed patients; depression in children. *J Affective Disord* 1988;2:1–16.

75. Pearlin LI, Lieberman MA. Social sources of emotional distress. In *Research in Community and Mental Health,* edited by Simmons R. Greenwich, Conn: JAI Press, 1977.

76. Fieve RR. *Moodswing.* New York: Bantam Books, 1975.

77. Elkin I, Pilkonis PA, Docherty JP, et al. Conceptual and methodological issues in comparative studies of psychotherapy and pharmacotherapy, I: active ingredients and mechanisms of change. *Am J Psychiatry* 1988;145:909–917.

78. Elkin I, Pilkonis PA, Docherty JP, et al. Conceptual and methodological issues in studies of psychotherapy and pharmacotherapy, II: nature and timing of treatment effects. *Am J Psychiatry* 1988;145:1070–1076.

79. Forrest T. The combined use of marital and individual therapy in depression. *Contemporary Psychoanal* 1969;6:76–83.

80. Bieber J. *Cognitive Psychoanalysis.* New York: Jason Aronson, 1980.

81. Regier DA, Hirschfeld RMA, Goodwin FK, et al. The NIMH

Depression Awareness, Recognition, and Treatment Program: structure, aims, and scientific basis. *Am J Psychiatry* 1988;145:1351–1357.

82. Akiskal HS. The bipolar spectrum: new concepts in classification and diagnosis. In *Psychiatry Update: The American Psychiatric Association Annual Review*, vol 2. Edited by Grinspoon L. Washington, DC: American Psychiatric Press, 1983.

83. Akiskal HS. The nosological status of neurotic depression. *Arch Gen Psychiatry* 1978;35:756–766.

84. Lesse S (ed). *Masked Depression*. New York: Jason Aronson, 1974.

85. Spitz R. *The First Year of Life*. New York: International Universities Press, 1965.

86. Weiner IB. Depression in adolescence. In *The Nature and Treatment of Depression*, edited by Flach FF, Draghi SC. New York: John Wiley & Sons, 1975.

87. Levinson D. *The Seasons of a Man's Life*. New York: Alfred A Knopf, 1978.

88. Goldfarb AI. Depression in the old and aged. In *The Nature and Treatment of Depression*, edited by Flach FF, Draghi SC. New York: John Wiley & Sons, 1975.

89. Carlson GA, Kashani JH. Phenomenology of major depression from childhood through adulthood: analysis of three studies. *Am J Psychiatry* 1988;145:1222–1225.

90. Klerman GL. Introduction to mood disorders. In *Treatments of Psychiatric Disorders: A Task Force Report of the American Psychiatric Association*, vol 3. Washington, DC: American Psychiatric Association, 1989.

91. May R, Angel E, Ellenberger H. *Existence: A New Dimension in Psychiatry and Psychology*. New York: Basic Books, 1958.

92. *A Psychiatric Glossary*, 3rd ed. Washington, DC: American Psychiatric Association, 1969.

93. Akiskal HS. Affective disorders. In *The Merck Manual of Diagnosis and Therapy*, 14th ed, vol II. Edited by Berkow R. Rahway, NJ: Merck Sharp & Dohme Research Laboratories, 1982.

94. Akiskal HS. Diagnosis and classification of affective disorders:

new insights from clinical and laboratory approaches. *Psychiatr Dev* 1983;2:123–160.

95. Zimmerman M, Spitzer RI. Melancholia: from DSM-III to DSM-III-R. *Am J Psychiatry* 1989;146:20–28.

96. Kraepelin E. *Manic-Depressive Insanity and Paranoia* (1985). Edinburgh: E & S Livingstone, 1921.

97. Bleuler E. *Dementia Praecox or The Group of Schizophrenias* (1911). New York: International Universities Press, 1950.

98. Perris C. Towards an integrating theory of depression focusing on the concept of vulnerability. *Integrative Psychiatry* 1987;5:27–39.

99. Andreasen NC, Grove WM, Maurer R. Cluster analysis and the classification of depression. *Br J Psychiatry* 1980;137:256–265.

100. Karasu TB. Psychotherapy and pharmacotherapy: toward an integrative model. *Am J Psychiatry* 1982;139:1102–1113.

101. Yager J. Psychiatric eclecticism: a cognitive view. *Am J Psychiatry* 1977;134:736–741.

102. Karasu TB. Psychotherapies: an overview. *Am J Psychiatry* 1977;134:851–863.

103. Marmor J. Recent trends in psychotherapy. *Am J Psychiatry* 1980;137:409–416.

104. Karasu TB. The specificity versus nonspecificity dilemma: toward identifying therapeutic change agents. *Am J Psychiatry* 1986;143:687–695.

105. Bursten B. Diagnostic framework. *Int Rev Psychoanal* 1978;5:2–31.

106. Karasu TB, Skodol AE. VIth axis for DSM-III: psychodynamic evaluation. *Am J Psychiatry* 1980;137:607–610.

107. Akiskal HS, Akiskal K. Reassessing the prevalence of bipolar disorders: clinical significance and artistic creativity. *Psychiatry and Psychobiology* 1988;3:29–36.

108. Schoenberg M, Miller MG, Schoenberg CE. The mind-body dichotomy reified: an illustrative case. *Am J Psychiatry* 1978;135:1224–1226.

109. Freud S. An outline of psycho-analysis (1940[1938]). In *Complete Psychological Works, standard ed*, vol 23. London, Hogarth Press, 1964.

110. Greenson R. *The Technique and Practice of Psychoanalysis*, vol I. New York: International Universities Press, 1967.

111. Semrad E, Klerman G. Discussion. In *Psychiatric Drugs*, edited by Solomon P. New York: Grune & Stratton, 1966.

112. Sarwer-Foner GL. *The Dynamics of Psychiatric Drug Therapy*. Springfield, Ill: Charles C Thomas, 1960.

113. Barondes SH. General discussion. In *Psychiatric Drugs*, edited by Solomon P. New York: Grune & Stratton, 1966.

114. Blackburn IM, Bishop S, Glen AIM, et al. The efficacy of cognitive therapy in depression: a treatment trial using cognitive therapy and pharmacotherapy, each alone, and in combination. *Br J Psychiatry* 1981;139:181–189.

115. Rush AJ, Watkins JT. Group versus individual cognitive therapy: a pilot study. *Cognitive Therapy and Research* 1981;5:95–103.

116. Beck AT, Hollon SD, Young JE, et al. Treatment of depression with cognitive therapy and amitriptyline. *Arch Gen Psychiatry* 1985;42:142–148.

117. Weissman M, Klerman G, Prusoff B, et al. The efficacy of psychotherapy in depression. In *Psychological Therapies*, edited by Spitzer RL, Klein DF. Baltimore: Johns Hopkins University Press, 1976.

118. DiMascio A, Weissman MM, Prusoff BA, et al. Differential symptom reduction by drugs and psychotherapy in acute depression. *Arch Gen Psychiatry* 1979;36:1450–1456.

119. Klerman GL, DiMascio A, Weissman M, et al. Treatment of depression by drugs and psychotherapy. *Am J Psychiatry* 1974;131:186–191.

120. Weissman MM, Myers JK, Thompson WD. Depression and its treatment in a US urban community, 1975–1976. *Arch Gen Psychiatry* 1981;38:417–421.

121. Weissman MM, Klerman GL, Prusoff BA, et al. Depressed outpatients: one year after treatment with drugs and/or interpersonal psychotherapy. *Arch Gen Psychiatry* 1981;38:51–55.

122. Rounsaville BJ, Klerman GL, Weissman MM. Do psychotherapy and pharmacotherapy conflict? *Arch Gen Psychiatry* 1981;38:24–29.

123. Weissman MM, Prusoff BA, Klerman GL. Personality and the prediction of long-term outcome of depression. *Am J Psychiatry* 1978;135:797–800.
124. Prusoff BA, Weissman MM, Klerman GL, et al. Research Diagnostic Criteria subtypes of depression: their role as predictors of differential response to psychotherapy and drug treatment. *Arch Gen Psychiatry* 1980;37:796–801.
125. Morris JB, Beck AT. The efficacy of antidepressant drugs. In *Progress in Psychiatric Drug Treatment*, vol 2, edited by Klein DF, Gittelman-Klein R. New York: Brunner/Mazel, 1976.
126. Mayer D. A psychotherapeutic approach to the suicidal patient. *Br J Psychiatry* 1971;119:629–633.
127. Bernstein JG. *Handbook of Drug Therapy in Psychiatry*. Boston: John Wright-PSG, 1983.
128. Klerman GL. Combining drugs and psychotherapy in the treatment of depression. In *Drugs in Combination With Other Therapies*, edited by Greenblatt M. New York: Grune & Stratton, 1975.
129. Halleck SL. *The Treatment of Emotional Disorders*. New York: Jason Aronson, 1978.
130. Prien RF. Somatic treatment of unipolar depressive disorder. In *American Psychiatric Press Review of Psychiatry*, vol 7, edited by Frances AJ, Hales RE. Washington, DC: American Psychiatric Press, 1988.
131. Prien RF, Caffey EM. Long-term maintenance drug therapy in recurrent affective illness: current status and issues. *Dis Nerv Syst* 1977;38:981–992.
132. Group for the Advancement of Psychiatry. *Pharmacotherapy and Psychotherapy: Paradoxes, Problems, and Progress: Report 93*. New York: GAP, 1975.
133. Shea MT, Elkin I, Hirschfeld RMA. Psychotherapeutic treatment of depression. In *American Psychiatric Press Review of Psychiatry*, vol 7, edited by Frances AJ, Hales RE. Washington, DC: American Psychiatric Press, 1988.
134. Weissman MM. The psychological treatment of depression: an update of clinical trials. In *Psychotherapy Research: Where Are We and Where Should We Go?* edited by Williams JBW,

Spitzer RL. New York: Guilford Press, 1984.

135. Covi L, Lipman RS, Derogatis LR, et al. Drugs and group psychotherapy in neurotic depression. Am J Psychiatry 1974;131:191–198.

136. Arieti S. A psychotherapeutic approach to severely depressed patients. Am J Psychother 1978;32:33–47.

137. Cadoret R, Winokur G. Genetic studies of affective disorders. In The Nature and Treatment of Depression, edited by Flach FF, Draghi SC. New York: John Wiley & Sons, 1975.

138. Paykel ES. Environmental variables in the etiology of depression. In The Nature and Treatment of Depression, edited by Flach FF, Draghi SC. New York: John Wiley & Sons, 1975.

139. Mendels J, Chernik DA. Sleep changes and affective illness. In The Nature and Treatment of Depression, edited by Flach FF, Draghi SC. New York: John Wiley & Sons, 1975.

140. Faragalla FF. Endocrine factors in depressive illness. In The Nature and Treatment of Depression, edited by Flach FF, Draghi SC. New York: John Wiley & Sons, 1975.

141. Sachar E. Endocrine factors in depressive illness. In The Nature and Treatment of Depression, edited by Flach FF, Draghi SC. New York: John Wiley & Sons, 1975.

142. Sifneos PE. Short-Term Dynamic Psychotherapy. New York: Plenum, 1979.

143. Gotlib IH, Asarnow RF. Interpersonal and impersonal problem-solving skills in mildly and clinically depressed university students. J Consult Clin Psychol 1979;47:86–95.

144. Rush AJ, Beck AT, Kovacs M, et al. Comparison of the effects of cognitive therapy and pharmacotherapy on hopelessness and self-concept. Am J Psychiatry 1982;139:862–866.

145. Simons AD, Lustman PJ, Wetzel RD, et al. Predicting response to cognitive therapy of depression: the role of learned resourcefulness. Cognitive Therapy and Research 1985;9:79–89.

146. Akiskal HS. Mood disturbances. In The Medical Basis of Psychiatry, edited by Winokur G, Clayton P. Philadelphia: WB Saunders, 1986.

147. Frank J. Persuasion and Healing: A Comparative Study of

Psychotherapy. Baltimore: Johns Hopkins University Press, 1961.

148. Strupp H. On the basic ingredients of psychotherapy. *Psychother Psychosom* 1974;24:249–260.

149. Elkin I, Shea MT, Watkins JT, et al. National Institute of Mental Health Treatment of Depression Collaborative Research Program: general effectiveness of treatments. *Arch Gen Psychiatry* 1989;46:971–982.

150. Smith ML, Glass GV, Miller TI. *The Benefits of Psychotherapy.* Baltimore: Johns Hopkins University Press, 1980.

151. Editorial note (especially for the media). *Arch Gen Psychiatry* 1989;46:983.

152. Burton R. *The Anatomy of Melancholy* (1621). New York: Dutton, 1961.

Index